GREAT MILITARY LEADERS
of the 20TH Century

Douglas MacArthur
Mao Zedong
George S. Patton
John J. Pershing
Erwin J.E. Rommel
H. Norman Schwarzkopf

DATE DUE

#47-0114 Peel Off Pressure Sensitive

GREAT
MILITARY LEADERS
of the 20TH Century

DOUGLAS MacARTHUR

EARLE RICE JR.

INTRODUCTION BY
CASPAR W. WEINBERGER

SERIES CONSULTING EDITOR
EARLE RICE JR.

CHELSEA HOUSE
PUBLISHERS
A Haights Cross Communications Company
Philadelphia

FRONTIS: **Side portrait of MacArthur**

CHELSEA HOUSE PUBLISHERS

VP, NEW PRODUCT DEVELOPMENT Sally Cheney
DIRECTOR OF PRODUCTION Kim Shinners
CREATIVE MANAGER Takeshi Takahashi
MANUFACTURING MANAGER Diann Grasse

STAFF FOR DOUGLAS MACARTHUR

EXECUTIVE EDITOR Lee Marcott
PRODUCTION ASSISTANT Megan Emery
PICTURE RESEARCHER Noelle Nardone
SERIES & COVER DESIGNER Keith Trego
LAYOUT 21st Century Publishing and Communications, Inc.

A Haights Cross Communications ✦ Company

http://www.chelseahouse.com

First Printing

1 3 5 7 9 8 6 4 2

Library of Congress Cataloging-in-Publication Data

Rice, Earle.
  MacArthur, general of the Army / Earle Rice, Jr.
    p. cm.—(Great military leaders of the twentieth century)
Summary: A look at the life and military accomplishments of General
Douglas MacArthur, whose career included serving as commander of
the U.S. Army Forces in the Far East during World War II. Includes
bibliographical references and index.
  ISBN 0-7910-7402-1 (hardcover)
  1. MacArthur, Douglas, 1880-1964—Juvenile literature. 2. Generals—
United States—Biography—Juvenile literature. 3. United States.
Army—Biography—Juvenile literature. 4. United States—History,
Military—20th century—Juvenile literature. [1. MacArthur, Douglas,
1880-1964. 2. Generals.] I. Title. II. Series.
E745.M3R49 2003
355'.0092—dc21
                                                    2003004743

TABLE OF CONTENTS

INTRODUCTION

by Caspar W. Weinberger

At a time when it is ever more apparent that the world will need skilled and bold military leaders, it is both appropriate and necessary that school history courses include studies of great military leaders.

Democracies, for the most part, are basically not greatly interested in military leadership or military matters in general. Fortunately, in the United States we have sufficient interest and volunteers for military service so that we can maintain and staff a very strong military with volunteers—people who want to serve.

That is very fortunate indeed for us. Volunteers and those who decide of their own free will that they want to be in the military are, generally speaking, easier to train, and to retain in the services, and their morale is markedly higher than that of conscripts. Furthermore, the total effect of a draft, based on our Vietnam experience, can be very bad—indeed it can polarize the country as a whole.

One of the best ways of ensuring that we will continue to have enough volunteers in the future is to study the great accomplishments of our past military leaders—the small group of leaders and others who contributed so much to our past greatness and our present strength.

Not all of these leaders have been Americans, but the

example that all of them set are well worth studying in our schools. Of the six military leaders chosen by Chelsea House's "Great Military Leaders of the 20th Century," I had the privilege of serving under and with two.

In World War II, after two years of volunteer service in the infantry at home and in the Pacific, I was transferred from the 41st Infantry Division then in New Guinea, to General Douglas MacArthur's intelligence staff in Manila, in the Philippines. One of my assignments was to prepare drafts of the general's daily communiqué to other theatre commanders around the world. This required seeing all of the major military cable and intelligence information, and digesting the most important items for his daily report to the other war theatres of the world. It also required a familiarity with our plans to carry the war to the enemy as soon as sufficient strength had been transferred to our theatre from Europe.

The invasion of Japan toward which all the planning was aiming would have been a very difficult and costly operation. Most of the tentative plans called for landing our force on one of the southern Japanese islands, and another force on Honshu, north of Tokyo.

We know that Japan's troops would have fought fiercely and very skillfully once their homeland was invaded. In fact, all of our plans forecast that we would lose virtually all of the first two U.S. divisions that landed. That was one of the main reasons that President Harry Truman concluded we had to use the atomic bomb. That ended the war, and all landings taken in Japan were peaceful and unopposed.

Many years later, when I was secretary of defense under President Ronald Reagan, a part of my duties was to recommend generals and admirals for various U.S. and NATO regional commands. Fulfilling this duty led me to interview several possible candidates for the post of commander in chief of our Central Command, which had jurisdiction over our many military activities in the Middle East.

My strong recommendation, accepted by the president, was that he name General H. Norman Schwarzkopf to lead the Central Command. A short time later, General Schwarzkopf led our forces in that region to the great military victory of the Gulf War.

General MacArthur and General Schwarzkopf shared many of the same qualities. Both were very experienced army officers tested by many widely different conditions all over the world. Both were calm, resolute, and inspirational leaders. Both were superb military planners and developers of complex and very large-scale military operations. Both achieved great military successes; both had the best interest of all our troops at heart; and both were leaders in the best sense of the word. They both had the ability and skills necessary to work with military and civilian leaders of our allies and friends in all parts of the globe.

It is vitally important for our future as a democracy, a superpower and a country whose strengths have helped save freedom and peace, that our children and our schools know far more about these leaders and countless others like them who serve the cause of peace with freedom so well and so faithfully. Their lives and the lives of others like them will be a great inspiration for us and for later generations who need to know what America at its best can accomplish.

The other military leaders whose lives are presented in this series include a German, General Erwin Rommel, and the former Communist China leader, Mao Zedong.

General Rommel won many preliminary battles in the desert war of World War II before losing the decisive battle of El Alamein. He had to develop and execute his tactics for desert fighting under conditions not previously experienced by him or his troops. He also became one of the masters of the art of tank warfare.

Mao Zedong had to train, develop, arm, and deploy huge numbers of Chinese soldiers to defeat the organized and experienced forces of Chiang Kai-shek's Nationalist government. He accomplished this and, in comparatively short time, won the military victories that transformed his country.

Both of these generals had to learn, very quickly, the new tactics needed to cope with rapidly changing conditions. In short, they had to be flexible, inventive, and willing and able to fight against larger opposing forces and in unfamiliar environments.

This whole series demonstrates that great military success requires many of the qualities and skills required for success in other fields of endeavor. Military history is indeed a vital part of the whole story of mankind, and one of the best ways of studying that history is to study the lives of those who succeeded by their leadership in this vital field.

CASPAR W. WEINBERGER
CHAIRMAN, *FORBES* INC
MARCH 2003

CASPAR W. WEINBERGER was the fifteenth U.S. secretary of defense, serving under President Ronald Reagan from 1981 to 1987, longer than any previous defense secretary except Robert McNamara (served 1961–1968). Weinberger is also an author who has written books about his experiences in the Reagan administration and about U.S. military capabilities.

1

"I Shall Return"

America's war with Japan was 79 days old when the presidential order began coming in on the radio at 11:23 A.M., February 23, 1942, Manila time. Cryptographers in the Malinta Tunnel on Corregidor Island decoded the message and delivered it to General Douglas MacArthur, the commander of the U.S. Army Forces in the Far East (USAFFE).

After Japan's surprise attacks on U.S. military installations at Pearl Harbor and in the Philippines in December 1941, the Japanese Fourteenth Army had landed and established itself in northern Luzon, the chief island of the Philippines. As the Japanese troops advanced southward toward Manila, the capital of the islands, MacArthur ordered his forces to withdraw into the

In the face of a Japanese invasion of the Philippines, President Franklin Roosevelt ordered General MacArthur (at right) to leave his field headquarters at Corregidor for the safety of Australia. Although MacArthur strongly disagreed with the president, he reluctantly withdrew. He pledged to return, however.

Bataan Peninsula. He then moved his headquarters from Manila to Fort Mills on Corregidor—a small, fortified island situated near the mouth of Manila Bay, two miles off the tip of the Bataan Peninsula.

From his headquarters on "the Rock," as Corregidor was more popularly known to American forces, MacArthur declared Manila an open city—that is, an undefended city protected from bombing by international law — to spare it from destruction. MacArthur subsequently vowed that he, along with his wife, Jean, and his four-year-old son, Arthur, would "share the fate of this garrison,"[1] meaning all the U.S.–Filipino troops under his command. Now, with the message handed to him at 12:30 P.M., U.S. President Franklin D. Roosevelt was ordering him to betray his vow:

> [T]he President directs that you make arrangements to leave Fort Mills and proceed to Mindanao [in the Philippines]. You are directed to make this change as quickly as possible. The President desires that in Mindanao you take such measures as will insure a prolonged defense of that region.[2]

The message went on to indicate that he was to spend no longer than a week in Mindanao before moving on to Australia to assume a new command. After reading the presidential order, MacArthur paled and seemed to those close to him to age ten years in the space of a few minutes. In private, he told his wife, Jean, "I am American-Army born and bred and accustomed by a lifetime of discipline to the obedience to superior orders. But this order I must disobey."[3] Then he wept.

That evening, MacArthur called his staff together and announced his decision to remain true to his vow. Rather than face a court-martial for disobeying orders, he told them, he would resign his commission, join his forces on Bataan, and enlist as "a simple volunteer."[4] He expected his staff to agree with his decision. They did not. Instead, they insisted that he owed it to his men to save himself for the continuing fight against Japan. After a night of soul-searching, MacArthur decided to accept their advice.

In a carefully drafted reply to the president the next day, MacArthur requested permission to delay his departure until the right "pyschological time,"[5] to be determined at his own discretion:

> I know the situation here in the Philippines and unless the right moment is chosen for this delicate operation, a sudden collapse might occur. . . . These people are depending on me now . . . and any idea that might develop in their minds that I was being withdrawn for any other purpose than to bring them immediate relief could not be explained.[6]

Army Chief of Staff General George C. Marshall approved MacArthur's request and authorized him to call on the navy and army commands in Australia for a submarine to take him to Mindanao and a B-17 bomber to fly him from there to Australia. Because of his reputed claustrophobic tendencies, however, MacArthur felt unreceptive to a 500-mile journey beneath the sea and called instead on the services of Lieutenant John D. "Buck" Bulkeley, commander of the U.S. Navy's Motor Torpedo Boat Squadron Three.

After three months of action without replacement parts, Bulkeley's original squadron of six PT (Patrol Torpedo) boats was by then reduced to four decrepit craft (PT-32, -34, -35, and -41). MacArthur asked Bulkeley if he could convey the evacuation party—the general himself, his wife and son, the boy's nanny, and 17 handpicked officers—across 500-plus miles of enemy-controlled waters, most of which were poorly charted or not charted at all. Bulkeley said he could. MacArthur—under constant pressure from the president to get started—finally set March 11, 1942, as the departure date for his party of 21 persons.

On March 10, MacArthur met for the last time with Major General Jonathan Wainwright, the gaunt commander of the North Luzon Force on Bataan. He informed Wainwright of his departure and turned over his USAFFE command to him. "I want you to make it known through-out all elements of your command that I am leaving over my repeated protests,"[7] he said. Wainwright said that he would, and MacArthur presented him with a box of cigars and two large jars of shaving cream.

"If I get through to Australia you know I'll come back as soon as I can with as much as I can," MacArthur said. "In the meantime, you've got to hold."[8] The two soldiers shook hands warmly and said good-bye. A distant murmur of artillery from Bataan filled in for words left unsaid.

PT Boats

PT (Patrol Torpedo) boats were small, fast torpedo craft used by the U.S. Navy in several combat zones during and after World War II. They were patterned after the MTBs (Motor Torpedo Boats) used by Great Britain and various other nations.

Because of the oceans isolating North America from potential enemies, the United States showed little interest in PT boats until the eve of World War II. Ironically, in 1937, General Douglas MacArthur became a leading proponent for the swift little craft that would successfully deliver him and his party from imminent capture by the Japanese in the Philippines several years later. In planning for the defense of the vast island group, MacArthur felt that a fleet of some 100 torpedo boats could repulse a potential Japanese invasion. A year later, the U.S. Congress authorized 5 million dollars for an experimental PT-boat program. After a competition and subsequent trials among three boatyards, the navy awarded contracts to both the Elco and Higgins yards to build the boats.

Specifications of the boats varied slightly but typically called for a length of 77 feet, a width of 20.7 feet, a draft of 5.3 feet, and a loaded weight of 46 tons. Three Packard gasoline engines powered the wood-hulled craft to a maximum speed of 41 knots (47.2 miles per hour). Armament consisted of four torpedoes plus two pairs of .50-caliber Browning machine guns. Crews, depending on boat model and mission, ranged from 11 to 17 personnel, generally two officers and the rest enlisted men.

"You'll get through,"[9] Wainwright replied.

"If you're still on Bataan when I get back," MacArthur promised, "I'll make you a lieutenant general."[10]

"I'll be on Bataan if I'm alive."[11]

On Wednesday, March 11, 1942, at 7:15 P.M., MacArthur walked across the porch of the gray cottage that had been his home on Corregidor and said gently to his wife, "Jean, it is time to go."[12] The MacArthurs and their Chinese nanny, Ah Cheu, drove to the island's South Dock, where Lieutenant Bulkeley and his boat awaited them. Three others assigned to PT-41 had already boarded the boat—MacArthur's chief of staff, Major General Richard K. Sutherland; his aide, Lieutenant Colonel Sidney L. Huff; and his doctor, Major Charles H. Morhouse.

To avoid drawing unwanted attention to MacArthur's party, the escape plan called for the other evacuees to depart from Mariveles and Sisiman Cove on Bataan. The four PT boats were to thread through the American-laid minefield at the mouth of Manila Bay and rendezvous offshore. They would then set a southerly course for Tagauayan, a small deserted islet in the unoccupied Cuyo Islands, expecting to arrive at about 7:30 the next morning. The boats would lay over there during the day, out of sight of Japanese aircraft, and await the arrival of the U.S. submarine *Permit* that night.

If MacArthur had changed his mind about submarines by then, the *Permit* would take him and his party on to Australia. If not, at 5:00 on the second night, all four boats would continue southwesterly to Cagayan, Mindanao, arriving at about 7:00 the following morning. At nearby Del Monte Field, four B-17s would be waiting to ferry them to Australia.

At 9:15 P.M., all four boats assembled on the seaward side of the minefield on a moonless night and formed into a diamond pattern. The PT-41 led off. If attacked, Bulkeley's

The original plan for MacArthur's withdrawal from the Philippines called for four B-17 bombers to pick up the general's party at Mindanao. Mechanical problems and the unforeseen crash of one plane, however, delayed MacArthur's arrival in Australia.

boat would try to escape while the other three boats engaged the enemy. Once formed, all four boats opened wide the throttles of their three-shaft, 4,050 horsepower Packard engines and sped south. The Rock quickly receded in froth and spray and seas that heaved ominously. "[T]he fate of Bataan was sealed," Colonel Huff recalled thinking later, "but we had little confidence that anything better awaited us at sea."[13]

As well-laid plans often do, the escape plan—along with all four boats—quickly went astray. In the heavy seas, the boats became separated during the night, and each proceeded alone to the appointed destination. Lieutenant (jg) V. S. Schumacher's PT-32 somehow sped ahead of the PT-41 in the darkness. At first light, Schumacher thought that he saw an enemy destroyer bearing down on him fast astern.

The young lieutenant jettisoned the extra gasoline drums that he would need to reach Mindanao and tried to outrun the pursuing vessel. When he could not, he swung about for a torpedo attack. Two of MacArthur's general officers cautioned him not to fire until he had positively identified the other vessel. Fortunately, Schumacher heeded their advice. Moments later—with a pair of torpedoes set to fire—Schumacher recognized the "destroyer" as Bulkeley's PT-41, "oddly magnified in the half-light of dawn."[14]

Although Bulkeley's party narrowly averted disaster from friendly fire, they were less successful at avoiding the seafarer's malady: Seasickness took a heavy toll on them. All but Jean and ex-navy man Huff fell deathly ill. MacArthur later likened the voyage to "a trip in a concrete mixer."[15] He began to give serious consideration to the advantages of transferring his party to the submarine *Permit* at Tagauayan.

Schumacher's decision to jettison his extra gasoline drums had left his boat with insufficient fuel to make it to Mindanao. Moreover, both boats had fallen behind schedule during the night. They could not reach Tagauayan without a long daylight run, so Bulkeley led them to a sheltered cove in another island of the Cuyo group. Lieutenant R.G. Kelly's PT-34 joined them there about two hours later. It was Thursday, March 12.

The three boats laid over—anxiously—all morning in the inlet. After seeing no sign of Japanese air or sea patrols, MacArthur decided that it was safe to move on. They reached Tagauayan at about 5:15 P.M. Ensign A.B. Aker's PT-35 never showed up there. MacArthur learned later that it had broken down with fouled gasoline strainers. Aker's boat eventually made it to Australia on its own.

At Tagauayan, MacArthur decided not to wait for the *Permit* but to continue on to Mindanao by boat. After transferring Schumacher's passengers to the 35 and 41 boats, and leaving the PT-32 at Tagauayan to await the *Permit*, MacArthur's party departed for Cagayan at 6:30 that night. (The PT-32 later developed engine trouble and leaks and had to be sunk by the *Permit* with cannon fire.) Shortly after their departure, while it was still daylight, PT-41's port lookout shouted, "Sail-ho! Looks like an enemy cruiser!"[16] It was indeed a cruiser—and the two torpedo boats were on a course that would carry them directly across its bow.

Bulkeley took quick evasive action and—with a lot of luck—managed to slip by the enemy warship unnoticed. "I think it was the whitecaps that saved us," he said. "The Japs didn't notice our wake, even though we were foaming away at full throttle."[17] A few minutes later, they narrowly escaped discovery by a Japanese destroyer. Still later, as the boats approached Negros Island after dark, a battery of enemy coastal artillery heard them. The Japanese, mistaking the roar of Packard engines for American warplanes, stabbed the sky with their searchlight beams, while the PT boats lumbered past offshore.

The two boats struggled on across the Mindanao Sea without further incident that night and made landfall near the Del Monte pineapple plantation at 6:30 A.M. on Friday, March 13. A half-hour or so later, MacArthur shook the salt spray from his gold-braided cap, reset it at a jaunty angle, and helped Jean ashore. Turning back toward the boats, he said, "Bulkeley, I'm giving every officer and man here the Silver Star [the nation's third-highest award] for gallantry. You've taken me out of the jaws of death, and I won't forget it."[18] MacArthur's gratitude turned abruptly to anger and indignation when he learned that there were no B-17s waiting at Del Monte Field to ferry his party to Australia.

Three of the four-engine bombers—old and failing survivors of the fighting in Java—had been sent to Mindanao. One turned back to Australia, one had crashed in the sea, and Brigadier General William F. Sharp, the

American commander on Mindanao, had rejected the third as unfit and ordered it back to Australia. MacArthur and his party waited three and a half days at Cagayan for the arrival of two reliable B-17s furnished by the U.S. Navy, while MacArthur fumed and Japanese troops in southern Mindanao advanced to the north. The party finally became airborne in the early hours of March 21.

En route to Darwin, the B-17 pilots twisted and dived and somehow managed to elude patrolling Japanese Zero fighters. Later, reports of Japanese bombers heading toward Darwin forced the B-17s to divert to Batchelor Field, about 50 miles south of Darwin, where they landed safely at 9:30 A.M. on March 17. Sid Huff called their five-day escape migration "a kind of miracle."[19]

At Batchelor Field, MacArthur and his party boarded an ancient narrow-gauge train for a four-day journey to Melbourne. They stopped briefly at Adelaide, where reporters greeted them for the first time. When asked for a statement, MacArthur said:

> The President of the United States ordered me to break through the Japanese lines and proceed from Corregidor to Australia for the purpose, as I understand it, of organizing the American offensive against Japan, a primary object of which is the relief of the Philippines. I came through and *I shall return.*[20]

And he would—but not soon enough for some 76,000 valiant defenders of Bataan and Corregidor.

2

First Ordeal by Fire

The nine years following MacArthur's miraculous escape from Corregidor would bring both fame and shame to the general whose battered gold-braided cap, Hollywood-style sunglasses, and upward-tilted corncob pipe endeared his cavalier image to millions of Americans. Many of the successes and some of the failures of this controversial leader derived directly from the influence of his extraordinary parents.

MacArthur's father, Arthur MacArthur Jr., established a staunch military tradition in the family. Arthur Jr. was born in Chicopee, Massachusetts, in 1845. Arthur Sr., a Scottish immigrant who prospered as a lawyer, a politician, and later as a distinguished federal judge in Washington, D.C., moved

As shown by this portrait, Douglas MacArthur (standing with a rifle on the left) was not the first military man in his family. His father, Arthur (seated), served the Union in the Civil War and was awarded the Medal of Honor for gallantry in action. His courage and tenacity earned him several battlefield promotions; he became a colonel within a year.

his family to Wisconsin when Arthur Jr. was four years old.

In 1862, at age 17, Arthur Jr. enlisted in the 24th Wisconsin Voluntary Infantry in Milwaukee. For the duration of the Civil War, he fought in battle after furious battle with uncommon courage and tenacity. On November 25, 1863, as a captain, he earned the Medal of Honor—his nation's highest award for gallantry in action—for his inspirational leadership on Missionary Ridge near Chattanooga, Tennessee.

At the base of the rebel-held ridge, under heavy plunging fire, Arthur Jr. grabbed the flagstaff of his regimental colors, leaped upward, and shouted, "On, Wisconsin!"[21] Charging to the crest of the hill, he stood silhouetted against the sky for all below to see. With his face blackened with smoke and his muddy uniform tattered and bloodstained, he planted the staff on the Confederate crest while his Wisconsin Bluecoats swarmed up and over the summit. Their action cleared the way for Sherman's march through Georgia.

Arthur's commanding officer noted in his report, "I think it is no disparagement of others to declare that he was the most distinguished in action on a field where many of the regiment displayed conspicuous gallantry, worthy of the highest praise."[22] Promotions came quickly to Arthur Jr. after Missionary Ridge, but because of governmental sloth and red tape, he did not receive his Medal of Honor until 27 years later.

After Missionary Ridge, Arthur Jr.—hereinafter Arthur—fought in 13 battles in four months during Sherman's march toward Atlanta and was elevated in quick succession to the brevet ranks of major, lieutenant colonel, and colonel within the year. (A brevet rank is one conferred upon a military officer without the corresponding pay of an equivalent regular rank.) His rapid rise before the age of 20 earned him the nickname "Boy Colonel of the West."[23]

After the Civil War, Arthur mustered out of the volunteer service in June 1865 but entered the army with the regular commission of second lieutenant in February 1866. The army upped his rank to first lieutenant on the day of his reenlistment and promoted him to captain the following July. For the next 23 years, he remained a captain, caught in the post-Civil War dearth of promotions. He served in a string of army posts—mostly in the West and Southwest—before regaining formerly held ranks and continuing up the craggy path to high command. In describing Arthur's duties many years later, Douglas noted that he "engaged in the onerous task of pushing Indians into the arid recesses of the Southwest and of bringing the white man's brand of law and order to the Western frontier."[24]

In February 1875, Arthur, while serving at Jackson Barracks in New Orleans, met the vacationing Mary Pinkney Hardy at a Mardi Gras ball. Mary, affectionately called "Pinky" by her family, was the daughter of a wealthy Virginia cotton broker and a strong, independent woman in her own right. The 30-year-old captain and the 22-year-old Norfolk belle with dark hair and alluring eyes experienced what they later recalled as "love at first sight."[25] The couple married at Riveredge, the Hardy plantation in Norfolk, on May 19, 1875.

Their union yielded three sons within the next three and a half years: Arthur III, Malcolm, and Douglas. Pinky returned to Riveredge for the birth of her first two sons, but she gave birth to Douglas at the Little Rock Barracks in Arkansas on January 26, 1880. Soon afterward, the family moved to Fort Wingate, New Mexico, near Gallup, where Malcolm died of measles at age six in 1883. Douglas would later write in his memoirs, "His loss was a terrible blow to my mother, but it seemed only to increase her devotion to Arthur [III] and myself. This tie was to become one of the dominant factors in my life."[26]

Pinky, who descended on both sides of her family from distinguished southern aristocratic stock that predated the American Revolution, adapted quickly to the rugged and austere life of a frontier soldier. She instilled in Douglas a solid sense of family pride and impressed upon him his responsibility to uphold his proud heritage. With her encouragement, he developed a love of history and read extensively, particularly the biographies of notable world leaders. An Episcopalian,

Pinky passed on to Douglas her own abiding sense of religion and taught him the importance of neatness and proper grooming. Not least, she repeatedly drummed into him the notion that someday he would become a great man like his father, thus implanting in him a strong sense of destiny.

At age six, Douglas received his first formal education at Fort Leavenworth, Kansas, in 1886. After three years there, by his own admission, his academic record fell short of superlative. "I was a poor student,"[27] he said. Nor did his scholastic aptitude astound anyone at Force Public School in Washington, D.C., following his father's promotion to major and transfer to the Adjutant General's Department. "I was only an average student,"[28] he noted later. In 1892, his brother Arthur received an appointment to the U.S. Naval Academy at Annapolis, Maryland, and left home.

A year later, the rest of the family moved to Arthur's new duty station at Fort Sam Houston, on the outskirts of San Antonio, Texas. Back in the West, Douglas experienced an academic awakening. His father enrolled Douglas — who was then 13 — in the West Texas Military Academy for his four years of high school. Douglas later described his academic epiphany in his memoirs:

> There came a desire to know, a seeking for the reason why, a search for the truth. Abstruse mathematics began to appear as a challenge to analysis, dull Latin and Greek seemed a gateway to the moving words of the leaders of the past, laborious historical data led to the nerve-tingling battlefields of the great captains, Biblical lessons began to open the spiritual portals of a growing faith, literature to lay bare the souls of men. My studies enveloped me, my marks went higher, and many of the school medals came my way. But I also learned how little such honors mean after one wins them.[29]

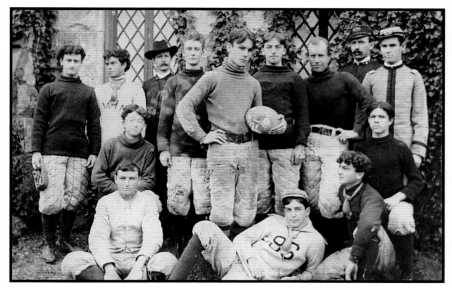

At the West Texas Military Academy, young Douglas MacArthur (number 96) excelled at sports. As quarterback, he led his football team to an undefeated season.

At the West Texas Military Academy, Douglas also excelled at athletics—tennis, baseball, and football. As a quarterback, he led his team to a perfect season. No opponent scored a single point against West Texas. Most important, his years at the academy kept him focused on the major aim of his young life: "Always before me was the goal of West Point," he wrote, "the greatest military academy in the world."[30] His brother Arthur, after graduating from the Naval Academy at Annapolis in 1896, quite likely thought otherwise.

Douglas finished his senior year at the top of his class with a grade average of 97.33. At graduation in 1897, he served as class valedictorian. The recognition and many awards that Douglas received at the academy in West Texas taught him a valuable lesson that he would carry with him for the rest of his life: Honors are fleeting and sustained only by continued achievement.

In October 1897, Arthur, now a lieutenant colonel, was posted to the Department of the Dakotas with headquarters in St. Paul, Minnesota. At the same time, Douglas and his mother checked in to a hotel in Milwaukee to establish residency in Representative Theobald Otjen's congressional district, where Douglas would study for the next year and a half for the competitive West Point examination. Arthur visited them on weekends.

On the night before the examination, Douglas could not sleep. On the morning of the test, he became nauseous. Pinky bolstered his confidence. "Doug, you'll win if you don't lose your nerve," she said. "You must believe in yourself, my son, or no one else will believe in you. Be self-confident, self-reliant, and even if you don't make it, you will know you have done your best. Now, go to it."[31] Douglas took the test and finished first among 13 applicants. His score stood at 99.33 compared to the next applicant's 77.9. The "cool words of my mother brought me around,"[32] he said.

Douglas entered West Point on June 13, 1899. The new plebe (freshman) flagged the immediate attention of his classmates, who recognized him as a leader from the start. His engaging physical appearance, along with his attractive features and his mother's dark hair and eyes, prompted one upperclassman to describe him as "without doubt the handsomest cadet that ever came into the academy, six-foot tall and slender, with a fine body and dark, flashing eyes."[33]

Pinky—his mother, his friend, and his confidante— moved into Craney's Hotel, at the edge of "the Plain," the broad shelf of land overlooking the Hudson River upon which stands the academy. She would stay there as a sort of "mother-in-residence" for the entire four years of her son's matriculation at West Point.

In the meantime, the Spanish-American War broke out

in April 1898, when the U.S. Congress recognized Cuba's right to independence and issued resolutions demanding the withdrawal of Spain's armed forces from the island. Arthur was promoted to brigadier general — skipping right

The Philippine Insurrection

In 1521, Ferdinand Magellan, a Portuguese navigator sailing for Spain, made landfall on the Philippine island of Cebu. Soon afterward, he met an untimely death on the nearby island of Mactan; but his around-the-world voyage opened the door to further Spanish exploration. By the end of the sixteenth century, Spain controlled most of the coastal and lowland areas of the Philippines — which were named for Philip II of Spain — from Luzon to northern Mindanao; Spain ruled the islands for the next 200 years.

Although the two-century Spanish rule was marked by numerous instances of Filipino resistance and unrest, the first armed revolt did not come until late in the nineteenth century. In 1892, Andres Bonifacio, a self-educated warehouseman, formed the nationalist Katipunan organization. "Katipunan" was a Filipino acronym for "Supreme Worshipful Association of the Sons of the People," a movement dedicated to Philippine Independence. Its membership numbered anywhere from 100,000 to 400,000 — mostly Tagalogs, the dominant cultural-linguistic group of central Luzon.

Fighting broke out prematurely around Manila in August 1896, when Spanish friars discovered a Katipunan plot to overthrow the Spanish government. Bonifacio proved to be an ineffectual military leader and was replaced by Emilio Aguinaldo, a local mayor. Aguinaldo concluded a truce with the Spaniards in December 1897 and was exiled to Hong Kong. When war broke out between the United States and Spain the next year, Aguinaldo returned to the Philippines and rallied his rebels to fight again against the Spaniards.

After the United States defeated Spain in the Spanish-American War of 1898, the Treaty of Paris ceded the Philippines to the United States. Aguinaldo and his followers saw this as an exchange of one imperialist government for another and took up arms against their former allies. The Philippine Insurrection — as the war against the Americans became known — ended officially in 1902, a year after Aguinaldo's capture, but scattered fighting continued in the islands for several more years.

over the rank of full colonel—and sent to fight in the Philippines. At the time, Arthur needed a map to learn the location of the islands.

Following Spain's surrender in Cuba in July 1898, Brigadier General Arthur MacArthur led 4,800 volunteers ashore at Cavite, south of Manila, on August 4. They were the vanguard of an 11,000-man expeditionary force under Major General Wesley Merritt. Arthur's contingent combined with the Filipino rebel forces of Emilio Aguinaldo to besiege Manila and force its Spanish captain-general to capitulate in nine days. U.S. casualties numbered 13 killed and 57 wounded. General Merritt praised the "outstanding" work of Arthur's volunteers and the "gallantry and excellent judgment"[34] of its brigadier.

Merritt rewarded Arthur by appointing him military governor of Manila, an honor that generated great pride among the MacArthur family, perhaps none greater than that of Arthur III. At the time of his father's appointment, Arthur III, who had fought in the Cuban naval action aboard the gunboat *Vixen* at Santiago, was stationed on a warship off Luzon. Although Douglas could not know it then, Luzon and the Philippines were fated to play an enormous role in his future.

Douglas, whose superb academic and athletic abilities had carried over from West Texas to West Point, graduated from the U.S. Military Academy at the top of his class on June 13, 1903, at the age of 23. During his four years at the academy, he accumulated a grade-point average of 98.14, won his "A" in athletics as a shortstop on the varsity baseball team, and earned the most coveted military honor of first captain of the Corps of Cadets.

As top man, Douglas was the first to take his place in "the Long Gray Line"—the procession of graduates that had begun with the first class in 1802—and to receive his certificate of graduation and commission as a second

When MacArthur applied for admission to West Point, he scored better than 99 percent on his exam, by far the best of 13 applicants in Milwaukee. Four years later, in 1903, he graduated at the top of his class.

lieutenant. Although Douglas favored the cavalry, he chose to serve in the Corps of Engineers, where promotions came faster. He was now ready to uphold the highest traditions of West Point, as represented in the three-word academy motto: Honor, Duty, Country. And Douglas knew exactly where he wanted to begin—in the Philippines.

After the Spanish-American War, the Treaty of Paris had transferred Philippine sovereignty from Spain to the United States in 1898. But followers of Emilio Aguinaldo sought Philippine independence and rebelled against U.S. rule. Arthur MacArthur, now a major general, commanded the principal field force against the rebels and was instrumental in quashing the Philippine Insurrection. Because of policy differences with William Howard Taft, who was then the first civilian governor of the Philippines, Arthur was transferred to the United States to head the army's Department of Colorado.

Although the Philippine Insurrection ended officially in 1902, sporadic guerrilla activity continued in the islands as late as 1906. In peacetime, advancement in the army comes fastest to those young officers who seek out the action wherever it can be found. For Douglas and nearly a dozen other members of West Point's Class of 1903, the action lay in the Philippines. In September 1903, Second Lieutenant Douglas MacArthur set sail for the islands from San Francisco and arrived in Manila 38 days later.

As an engineer in the Philippines, Douglas took part in numerous routine duties in the land that had made his father famous—surveying, undertaking various construction projects, even leading patrols. On one assignment, he helped to survey the Bataan Peninsula on Luzon.

In November 1903, on another assignment on the island of Guimaris, he led a detachment into the jungle to find timber for pilings and was ambushed by two insurrectionists. A sharp *crack!* pierced the forest stillness, and a bullet tore a hole through the crown of his campaign hat and slammed into a tree. Douglas drew his .38 pistol and answered his attackers. "Like all frontiersmen, I was an expert with a pistol," Douglas declared later. "I dropped them both dead in their tracks."[35]

After the brief—but deadly—encounter, an Irish sergeant inspected the dead bodies, then faced and saluted the 23-year-old officer. "Begging the lieutenant's pardon," he said, "but all the rest of the lieutenant's life is pure velvet!" [36] The young West Pointer had faced his first ordeal by fire and had met it smoothly.

Mexican Adventure

Soon after his clash with guerrillas in the Guimaris jungle, Douglas contracted malaria and was sent back to Manila. Though beset with fever from the disease, he still managed to pass the examination for first lieutenant and was elevated to that rank. After recovering from his fever, he was ordered to survey Mariveles, the tip of the Bataan Peninsula. On this assignment, he acquired a familiarity with the region that would serve him well many years later.

In October 1904, Douglas's recurring bouts with malaria cut short his tour of duty in the Philippines, and he received orders back to San Francisco. Before leaving the islands, however, he met and became friends with Manuel Quezon and Sergio

Douglas and his father Arthur (seen here) had the opportunity to serve together as observers after the Russo-Japanese War in 1905. The experience familiarized young Douglas with the structure and customs of the Japanese military.

Osmeña, both future presidents of the Philippine commonwealth. In less than a year, Douglas had gained valuable knowledge of the Philippines, and he had sown the seeds of an enduring relationship between himself and the Filipinos based on mutual affection and respect.

The 7,083-island Philippine archipelago had worked its magic on Douglas. "[T]he languorous laze that seemed to glamorize even the most routine chores of life, the fun-loving men, the moonbeam delicacy of its lovely women, fastened me with a grip that has never relaxed,"[37] he wrote later.

Back in San Francisco, Douglas was assigned to the

Golden Gate harbor defenses, and to the California Debris Commission, which was charged with clearing up the messes left by placer miners in the foothills of the Sierra Nevada. (Placer miners used various winnowing and earth removal methods—including gold panning and dredging—to separate valuable minerals from alluvial, or stream-bed, deposits. The miners and their methods often caused severe environmental damage.) Although he spent much of the year fighting off malarial relapses, he particularly enjoyed his work with the commission. "These duties were pleasant ones," he noted, "especially the stagecoach trips through the Strawberry Valley that recalled my early days in the West."[38] Meanwhile, U.S. President Theodore Roosevelt had sent Arthur (with Mrs. MacArthur) to the Far East to observe the Russo-Japanese War (1904–1905).

In October 1905, Douglas suddenly received orders to report for duty in Japan as his father's aide. He arrived in Yokohama in November, eight months after the end of the war. Arthur and his son now faced the task of evaluating the Japanese military. Douglas, after meeting the top echelon of Japanese commanders, described them as "grim, taciturn, aloof men of iron character and unshakable purpose" and was further impressed by the "boldness and courage"[39] of the common Japanese soldier. He quickly recognized the Japanese preoccupation with expanding beyond their borders. "Having conquered Korea and Formosa [Taiwan], it was more than evident that they would eventually strike out for control of the Pacific and domination of the Far East,"[40] he wrote later.

When the MacArthurs concluded their work in Japan, Washington ordered them to extend their intelligence-gathering mission to the entire Far East, including the Chinese mainland and India. For the next nine months, Douglas and his father—in company with Pinky—traversed the Orient and beyond. Father and son dutifully reported on their findings in Hong Kong, Singapore, Rangoon, Calcutta, Bombay, Java, Siam (Thailand), Indochina (Vietnam), and Shanghai. These exotic locales enchanted the young lieutenant and seemed to exert a "mystic hold"[41] on him. This journey to faraway places provided a rare opportunity for him to discover new vistas—to see and to learn.

At journey's end, Douglas observed, "It was crystal clear to me that the future, indeed the very existence of America, were irrevocably entwined with Asia and its island outposts."[42] He was beginning to form a worldview that would carry him to the pinnacle of his career. The MacArthurs returned to the United States in the summer of 1906. After their tour of Asia, neither Arthur nor Douglas expected another posting that could match the allure of world travel; neither man got one.

Arthur was promoted to lieutenant general—so becoming the senior officer in the army—and appointed head of the Department of the Pacific in San Francisco. He had hoped for an appointment as chief of staff of the army, but his criticisms of the War Department and his quarrels with William Howard Taft, who was now Secretary of War, frustrated his selection. He later turned down command of the Department of the East and retired in Milwaukee on June 2, 1909.

In the fall of 1906, Douglas reported as a student to an advanced engineering school in Washington, D.C. That winter, when classes were not in session, he served as a special aide to President Theodore Roosevelt. "The assignment proved of the greatest interest to me," he recalled, "since I came into close contact for the first time with the leading political figures of the country."[43] Serving among the Washington power brokers provided him with another heady experience.

Upon graduation in August 1907, after a short assignment on river and harbor duty in Wisconsin, Douglas was posted to Fort Leavenworth, Kansas, where he served for four and a half years as a company commander in the Third

Battalion of Engineers and later as the battalion's adjutant (administrative officer). He also served as a lecturer (instructor) at the General Service and Cavalry Schools at Fort Riley, Kansas. His efforts earned him a captaincy on February 27, 1911.

During this period (about 1910), an undiagnosed illness struck his mother, and a stroke claimed the life of his father on September 2, 1912. Douglas was shattered by his father's death. Moreover, with his brother Arthur III serving at sea, it fell to Douglas—hereinafter MacArthur—to care for the ailing Pinky, who was left alone in Milwaukee. MacArthur requested a transfer to the Washington area, near Johns Hopkins Hospital, so that his mother could receive the best of care.

In early 1913, MacArthur was posted to Washington as a member of the Engineer Board, and later as a general staff officer. Pinky came to live with him in a comfortable house in a fashionable Washington area. For both mother and son, the change offered an environment that was both uplifting and challenging. Pinky's mysterious illness soon disappeared, and her son was now well positioned to commence his long, steady climb to the top of his profession.

An opportunity for Captain MacArthur to distinguish himself arose the following year. In 1914, General Victoriano Huerta seized power from the regime of President Francisco Madera in Mexico and began harassing and arresting American citizens who were in that country legally. U.S. President Woodrow Wilson countered Huerta's intentional and repeated affronts to U.S. citizens by blockading the Mexican port of Veracruz and seizing the city with American sailors and marines on April 21. Wilson backed this action by dispatching the Fifth Brigade, a small expeditionary force under Major General Frederick Funston, to Veracruz. If necessary, a field army led by Major General Leonard Wood was to follow.

On April 22, General Wood summoned MacArthur to

his office and informed him that he had been selected for a special reconnaissance mission. As MacArthur would write later, he was to proceed "to Veracruz to study the lay of the land, and observe and report on all matters that might be useful to General Wood and the War Department."[44] MacArthur left for Veracruz an hour later.

When MacArthur arrived in Veracruz, he was alarmed to learn that the American brigade had little knowledge of

Veracruz

In 1913, General Victoriano Huerta deposed and replaced Mexican President Francisco Madera. Upon the assassination of Madera shortly afterward, a full-scale civil war broke out between Huerta's forces and those of General Venustiano Carranza, leader of the so-called Constitutionalists, and Emiliano Zapata, chief of the radicals. U.S. President Woodrow Wilson refused to recognize Huerta on the premise that his assumption of power did not stand the test of "constitutional legitimacy." Accordingly, Wilson imposed an arms embargo on both sides in the civil war.

When Huerta's forces succeeded in halting the Constitutionalists, Wilson lifted the embargo so that arms could reach the rebels. In February 1914, angered by Wilson's intervention, Huerta's followers arrested American sailors in the port of Tampico. Huerta soon expressed his regret and ordered the release of the sailors, but the commander of the U.S. fleet in the area demanded a public apology. Huerta refused. When a German freighter carrying arms and munitions arrived unexpectedly at Veracruz in late April, the U.S. fleet put ashore a contingent of sailors and marines to prevent unloading of the ship.

The Mexicans counterattacked, but naval gunfire kept them in check. By the end of the month, an American force of about 8,000 U.S. soldiers and marines under Major General Frederick Funston landed in Veracruz and occupied the city. For a time, war with Mexico loomed large but was avoided when both Huerta and Wilson agreed to mediation that resulted in the Mexican leader's resignation. Venustiano Carranza replaced Huerta but was himself immediately challenged by Francisco "Pancho" Villa, who rebelled and seized control of most of northern Mexico. But that is a tale for another time.

what the route to Mexico City was like, or of where the bulk of Huerta's troops was positioned. He also found the brigade lacking in mechanized transport. The American field army, if it came, would have to rely entirely on animals. Hundreds of boxcars were available in Veracruz, but there were no locomotives to haul them. MacArthur learned through rumors that Huerta's forces had hidden several locomotives behind enemy lines. He hired a Mexican guide and set out at once behind those lines on a self-assigned mission to find the locomotives.

MacArthur's subsequent report of the mission reads like pulp fiction. With the aid of his guide and a pair of Mexican railroad men whom he bribed, MacArthur proceeded inland to Alvarado, about 35 miles beyond Funston's lines. He found five locomotives, three of which "were just what we needed—fine big road pullers in excellent condition except for a few minor parts which were missing."[45] MacArthur started back to Veracruz with the news, and his troubles began.

Accosted by five armed men in Salinas, MacArthur "was obliged to fire upon them" and both "went down."[46] Later, at Piedra, his little party ran into 15 mounted men of similar character. He "was knocked down by the rush of horsemen and had three bullet holes in [his] clothes, but escaped unscathed."[47] MacArthur shot four of them and the rest fled. Still later, near Laguna, three more bandits attacked him. Another bullet pierced his shirt and two others struck within six inches of him. MacArthur returned fire and dropped his seventh foe. He and his party reached Veracruz without further incident.

General Wood recommended MacArthur for the Medal of Honor, citing that he had undertaken the expedition "at the risk of his life" and "on his own initiative," which showed "enterprise and courage worthy of high commendation."[48] But the War Department denied the award

After the overthrow of the Mexican president by rebels in 1914, Major General George Leonard Wood (seen here) ordered MacArthur to Mexico. Surviving several brushes with death, MacArthur was able to find three desperately needed locomotives behind enemy lines.

because MacArthur had not apprised General Funston of his reconnaissance. MacArthur filed for a review but was again denied the award.

After his Mexican adventure, MacArthur returned to Washington and resumed his duties on the general staff. He did not realize it at the time, but he was in the right place at the right time—and now on a fast track to high command.

4

"The Greatest Frontier General"

On June 28, 1914, barely more than a month after MacArthur's return to his War Department duties, a Serbian national assassinated Archduke Franz Ferdinand and his spouse in the Bosnian capital of Sarajevo. The slaying of the archduke, who was the heir to the Austro-Hungarian throne, triggered the outbreak of World War I. The great powers of Europe split along lines of long-standing alliances: the Central Powers, chiefly Germany and Austria-Hungary; and the Allied Powers or Allies, mainly France, Great Britain, and Russia. These opposing nations entered into the Great War (World War I).

The United States remained neutral, but the likelihood of its future involvement was never far removed from the thinking

40

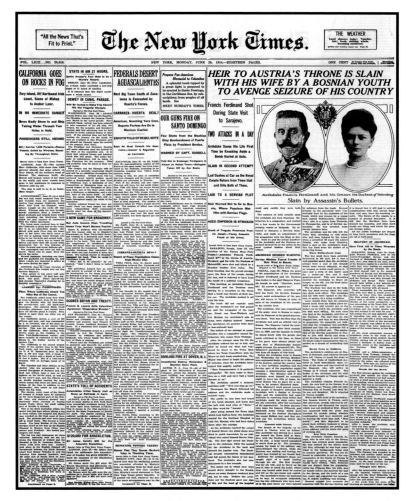

The 1914 assassination of Austria's Archduke Franz Ferdinand plunged Europe into World War I. Although at first it remained neutral, the United States entered the war in 1917. MacArthur was promoted from major to colonel and headed for France, where he led the now-famous "Rainbow Division."

of the American military. On December 11, 1915, MacArthur pinned on the gold leafs of a major. The following June, he was assigned as military assistant to Secretary of War Newton D. Baker and appointed head of the Bureau of Information of the War Department.

The two men developed a great mutual respect and worked closely together in preparing the army for a war that seemed certain to come.

In his new role, Major MacArthur became a champion of the new National Guard units. He succeeded in convincing both Secretary Baker and President Wilson that the guard units could fight effectively alongside regular army units in Europe if the United States became involved in the war. Germany's use of the submarine against neutral shipping removed the "if" from the question of U.S. involvement, and America joined the war on the side of the Allies in April 1917.

MacArthur, as might be expected of a West Pointer, itched to get into action against the Germans right away. He suggested forming a division from National Guard units from several states. Brigadier General William A. Mann, who headed the department's militia bureau, observed that guardsmen could be drawn from as many as 26 states. "Fine," MacArthur said, "that will stretch over the whole country like a rainbow."[49] A division was quickly formed from these diverse elements and activated as the Forty-Second Division, but it would always be better known as the "Rainbow" Division.

General Mann was named to command the Rainbow Division. Since Mann was nearing retirement age, MacArthur advised Secretary Baker to appoint the best colonel in the army as Mann's chief of staff. Baker put his hand on MacArthur's shoulder and said, "I have already made my selection for that post. It is you."[50] A flabbergasted MacArthur stammered that he did not qualify for the post, as he was only a major. "You are wrong," Baker replied, "You are now a colonel. I will sign your commission immediately. I take it you will want to be in the Engineer Corps."[51]

MacArthur, still stunned, said, "No, the Infantry." And

that is how MacArthur, as he put it himself later, "became a doughboy [infantryman]."[52] In October 1917, he left for France with the Forty-Second Rainbow Division, one of the forerunners of General John J. "Black Jack" Pershing's American Expeditionary Force (AEF).

In France, MacArthur gained fame for both his distinctive dress and daring deeds. He refused to wear a metal helmet or a gas mask. Typically, he wore a floppy cap, a bright-colored turtleneck sweater, always-neat khaki, and spotless puttees (leggings). He was seldom seen without his riding crop. Journalists soon dubbed him "the Beau Brummel of the AEF"[53] after a nineteenth-century English dandy. His choice of unorthodox attire only contributed to his distinctive image as premier leader of men. He could always be found in front of his troops in the thick of the fighting.

MacArthur fought in the Aisne-Marne Offensive (July 25–August 2, 1918) and was elevated to the brevet rank of brigadier general. As commander of the Eighty-Fourth Brigade, he distinguished himself during the St.-Mihiel Offensive (September 12–17). At age 38, during the ensuing Meuse-Argonne Offensive (October 4–November 11), he became the youngest division commander of the war when he led the Rainbow Division in the "race to Sedan" (November 6–11) to cut off a vital German railroad supply line.

MacArthur's first battle experience came on February 26, 1918, as a volunteer with a French raiding party. He found the action "savage and merciless."[54] His party captured 600 Germans. The French awarded him the croix de guerre (cross of war) for his part in the fighting. It was his first decoration. His own army pinned the Silver Star on him later for the same action.

In early March, MacArthur—although chiefs of staff are generally not disposed to frontline action—led a battalion of the 168th Infantry in an attack on a German salient (bulge in the lines) in the Lorraine sector. He recalled the action later in his memoirs:

> I went over the top as fast as I could and scrambled forward. The blast [from exploding enemy shells] was like a fiery furnace. For a dozen terrible seconds I felt that they [his troops] were not following me. But then, without turning around, I knew how wrong I was to have doubted for even an instant. In a moment they were around me, ahead of me, a roaring avalanche of glittering steel and cursing men. We carried the enemy position.[55]

From then on, the Rainbow Division held the utmost respect of both their allies and their enemies. MacArthur earned the Distinguished Service Cross—second only to the Medal of Honor for gallantry in action—for his part in the action. In another incident at the front on March 11, he was "slightly gassed"[56] and received the Purple Heart medal (awarded to those wounded in action against the enemy). MacArthur was well on his way to becoming one of the best-known American soldiers in France.

The Forty-Second Rainbow Division served in the front lines in the Lorraine sector under French General Pierre-Georges Duport for about four months. On June 21, the division was withdrawn from the lines for a rest. General Duport cited the Americans for their "offensive ardor, the spirit of method, the discipline shown by all its officers and men."[57] Five days later, on June 26, MacArthur received a telegram from Washington informing him of his promotion to brigadier general.

On July 4, the division returned to action in the Champagne sector under French General Henri Gouraud. Allied intelligence had learned that the Germans under General

MacArthur's flamboyant style and fierce leadership soon landed him the rank of brigadier general. This portrait from World War I shows the general seated in a throne-like chair so large that his feet do not touch the ground.

Erich von Ludendorff were planning to launch an all-out offensive in a desperate attempt to split the British and French armies and win the war. The Germans struck on July 15.

Parisians could hear the rumble of artillery from nearly 100 miles distant. For the next three days, battalions of gray-clad Germans swarmed across the scarred earth of No Man's Land, only to be turned away again and again by the Franco-American forces. On the third day, General Gouraud sent his compliments to MacArthur: "The German has clearly broken his sword against our lines. Whatever he may do in the future, he shall not pass."[58] And he did not.

MacArthur summed up the action later: "In a few spots they broke through, but in the main were repulsed and driven back. We launched counterattacks and . . . the outcome was clear—the German's last great attack of the war had failed, and Paris could breathe again."[59] For his part in stopping the German drive, MacArthur emerged from the battlefield with his second and third Silver Stars.

In recommending the new brigadier for the award, Major General Charles D. Menoher, who had succeeded the ailing Mann as commander of the Rainbow Division, wrote, "MacArthur is the bloodiest fighting man in this army. I'm afraid we're going to lose him sometime, for there's no risk of battle that any soldier is called upon to take that he is not liable to look up and see MacArthur at his side."[60]

On July 25, 1918, the Allies seized the initiative and launched the Aisne-Marne Offensive. Two days later, MacArthur earned his fourth Silver Star in front of Château-Thierry, in an action in which he used Indian tactics recalled from frontier tales of his youth. "Crawling forward in twos and threes against each stubborn nest of enemy guns, we closed in with the bayonet and the hand grenade," he wrote later. "It was savage and there was no quarter asked or given."[61]

After four days and nights of fierce fighting, in which MacArthur remembered not sleeping at all, the French and Americans broke through the German lines and drove deep into their territory. The French decorated MacArthur with a second croix de guerre and made him a commander in the Legion of Honor, France's highest-ranking commendation for extraordinary military bravery and service in times of war.

After the push in the Aisne-Marne sector, the Rainbow Division retired to a rest area in August. During the respite, MacArthur was shifted from chief of staff of the division to command of its Eighty-Fourth Infantry Brigade. On September 10, the division returned to the front to join the U.S. First Army's attack on the salient at St.-Mihiel—a bulge in the Allied lines that the Germans had held since 1914. With MacArthur leading the way, his brigade quickly achieved its object—and more. At St.-Mihiel, and in subsequent fighting, MacArthur earned his fifth and sixth Silver Stars for gallantry.

In early September, the Allies launched the Meuse-Argonne Offensive, the last great operation of the war. A month later, MacArthur's brigade, which now formed a part of the U.S. V Corps, was ordered to seize the German stronghold at Côte-de-Châtillon, the pivot of the entire Hindenburg Line, a 300-mile-long German defensive system made up of five major lines. MacArthur commenced his attack on the night of October 11.

Although gassed again and almost blinded in the first day's fighting, MacArthur continued to direct his brigade as it battled into the next day and early evening. Two of his battalions executed a pincer movement and enveloped their

After a successful yet brutal campaign at Aisne-Marne, MacArthur was given command of the 84th Infantry Brigade, where he soon added to his collection of Silver Stars.

objective from opposing sides. Blood and gore defined the action. In MacArthur's words:

> Officers fell and sergeants leaped to the command. Companies dwindled to platoons and corporals took over. At the end, Major Ross [one of MacArthur's battalion commanders] had only 300 men and 6 officers left out of 1,450 men and 25 officers. That is the way the Côte-de-Châtillon fell.[62]

Fifth Corps commander Brigadier General Charles P. Summerall, recommended MacArthur for the Medal of Honor—his second recommendation in three years—and promotion to major general. But the War Department again turned him down for the nation's premier award, and the Armistice in November froze all promotions. MacArthur had to settle for second awards of the Distinguished Service Cross and the Purple Heart.

After another brief rest, November 4 found the Forty-Second Rainbow Division back on line and advancing on Sedan, three miles to its front. Sedan held great symbolic and sentimental significance to the French because of France's crowning defeat there in the Franco-Prussian War of 1870. General Pershing had originally deferred its capture to his French allies. But when the French Fourth Army lagged behind the advancing American army, he issued an unclear message redefining the boundaries of advance. He had meant for the U.S. First Division to capture Sedan, but in the resulting confusion he had effectively put the Rainbow Division on a collision course with the U.S. First Division. In what became known as the "race to Sedan," an odd tragedy was narrowly averted.

When MacArthur learned of the presence of First Division elements in his sector, he hurried to the front to head off a possible exchange of friendly fire. At the front, a Sixteenth Infantry patrol confronted him. Because of his unusual attire—he was then wearing a floppy hat, muffler, riding breeches, and polished boots—the patrol leader mistook him for an enemy officer. He took MacArthur prisoner at pistol point and marched him back to headquarters. Fortunately, no shots were fired, and MacArthur was properly identified—but it was a close call. For the odd incident, MacArthur received his seventh Silver Star, the last of his World War I decorations.

On November 6, with the Germans in full retreat and

the war winding down, General Menoher was upgraded to corps command and MacArthur assumed command of the Rainbow Division. "On leaving the Rainbow, [Menoher] dispatched a most laudatory letter to General Pershing regarding my service under him and sent a copy to my mother," MacArthur noted later. "She cherished it to the day of her death, saying it was the greatest gift she had ever received."[63]

The Armistice came on November 11, 1918. Both the Rainbow Division and its last commander in World War I

A Mother's Influence

As the spouse of the senior officer in the U.S. Army and the product of a distinguished pre-Revolutionary southern heritage, Mary "Pinky" Hardy MacArthur held considerable sway in military and political circles. She never missed a chance to use her influence in furthering the careers of her sons, Arthur III and Douglas. She particularly focused on Douglas's army career.

Again and again, Pinky drummed into Douglas that it was nothing short of his duty to grow up to be a great man like his father—or like Robert E. Lee. To this end, she lovingly educated him in his youth in the ways of a gentleman, and she tutored him past the entrance examination for West Point in his adolescence. During Douglas's four-year matriculation at West Point, Pinky took up residence outside the academy to be near her son if needed. She was his friend, his confidante, and his rock-solid source of strength.

In 1917, when Douglas went to war as chief of staff with the Rainbow Division, Pinky initiated a one-woman campaign to get her son promoted to brigadier general. She wrote letters to Secretary of War Newton D. Baker and to American Expeditionary Force commander General John J. "Black Jack" Pershing, exerting her influence and urging her son's ascendancy. Douglas received word of his elevation to brigadier in the aftermath of Pinky's letter campaign.

Beyond question, Douglas warranted the promotion on his own merits alone, and no conclusive evidence ties Pinky's campaign to her son's advancement. But his mother's influence probably did not hurt.

had acquitted themselves nobly. The division served at the front for 224 days—162 of them in serious combat—and suffered 14,683 casualties, including 2,713 dead.

Douglas MacArthur had made his mark as unquestionably the finest West Pointer and one of the most highly decorated officers to emerge from the war. When the sounds of war faded into history, his phenomenal array of medals consisted of two Distinguished Service Crosses, seven Silver Stars, two Purple Hearts, and several French and numerous other foreign decorations. Secretary of War Newton Baker called his former protégé "the greatest frontier general"[64] of World War I. The secretary was not one to exaggerate.

5

"This Is My Destiny"

When "the War to End All Wars" ended, MacArthur remained in Germany for a brief tour of occupation duty. On March 16, 1919, General Pershing reviewed the Forty-Second Division on a plain near Remagen. He used the occasion to pin the Distinguished Service Medal on MacArthur to reward his achievements as the Rainbow's chief of staff. (The DSM is the highest decoration awarded to staff officers.) Soon afterward, Pinky, now 66, developed another of her mysterious illnesses. MacArthur requested—and got—a speedy return to the United States to be near his sick mother.

When the steamer *Leviathan* docked in New York on April 25, the first one off the ship was Brigadier General Douglas

During the occupation of Germany after World War I, MacArthur was awarded the Distinguished Service Medal by General John "Black Jack" Pershing, Here, Pershing is seen leaving the ship _Leviathan_ in New York upon his return to the United States.

MacArthur. Over his tunic, he wore a massive raccoon coat and a new scarf knitted by his mother. When reunited with her son, Pinky's illness took a remarkable turn for the better.

Soon after MacArthur's return stateside, army chief of staff General Peyton C. March summoned him to Washington, D.C. March, an old friend of MacArthur's father, said, "Douglas, things are in great confusion at West Point. . . . We want you to go up there and revitalize and revamp the academy."[65] MacArthur, shocked, protested that he was a field soldier and not an educator. He told March that he could not do it. "You can do it,"[66] March assured him.

The chief of staff offered MacArthur two choices: If he accepted the assignment, his wartime brevet rank of brigadier general would be confirmed as a commission in the regular army; if he refused it, his prewar rank of major would be reinstated. MacArthur arrived at West Point on June 12, 1919, to begin his new assignment at the academy. Pinky arrived with him, and mother and son moved into the superintendent's mansion of brick and iron grille.

MacArthur faced a tough task. Because of the accelerated need for officers during the war, the academy's course of instruction had been reduced to one year, and all of its upperclassmen had gone off to war. Only the freshman class remained. Further, the American public was weary of war and in no mood to finance the academy's reformation. Some congressmen even wanted to abolish West Point. But the new superintendent soon warmed to his task.

For the next three years, MacArthur struggled with an assortment of factions that held a vested interest in the school—politicians, the military, the faculty, the corps of cadets, and others. Despite the obstacles that confronted him, he succeeded magnificently in restoring—and improving—the academy as a leading institution of military learning.

Dr. D. Clayton James, MacArthur's preeminent early biographer, sums up his subject's performance this way: "Many aspects of MacArthur's long career are still controversial, but in the Long Gray Line [of academy graduates], there is general agreement that he, more than any other man, led West Point across the threshold into the rapidly changing world of modern military education."[67] For the second time, MacArthur turned in a stellar performance at West Point.

In September 1921, MacArthur's world wobbled and shook in its orbit: During a party at Tuxedo Park, about 20 miles south of the academy, the general met Henriette Louise Cromwell Brooks. Louise (she hated her first name) was a short, round-faced, 31-year-old divorcée with seductive brown eyes, tousled short hair, and an impish grin. She was also heir to a $150-million fortune (worth more than a billion dollars today). MacArthur fell for her like a rock in a pond. Apparently, it was the first time that he had ever been in love. He asked her to marry him before the night ended.

"If he hadn't proposed the first time we met," Louise told reporters later, "I believe I would have done it myself."[68] Pinky suffered the news of her son's betrothal predictably: She fell ill. Notwithstanding Pinky's disapproval, her son married the puckish heiress on St. Valentine's Day, 1922.

Earlier, in the summer of 1921, General Pershing had succeeded Peyton March as army chief of staff. Pershing, a widely known womanizer, had engaged in a brief affair with Louise in Paris after the war. Louise later became involved with Pershing's handsome aide, 38-year-old Colonel John G. Quekemeyer, who intended marriage with her. Pershing thought of Quekemeyer as a son and became angered when Louise broke off her relationship with the colonel.

In November 1921, Pershing informed MacArthur that he would be posted for overseas duty in the Philippines at the close of the academic year. Purportedly, Pershing's displeasure with Louise had nothing to do with MacArthur's transfer after serving only three years of a usual four-year term as superintendent at West

Point. In any event, MacArthur and Louise, and Louise's two children, departed San Francisco for the Philippines in September 1922 aboard the transport *Thomas*.

"It was early in October 1922 when the transport *Thomas* docked Pier Five in Manila," MacArthur wrote later, "and once again the massive bluff of Bataan, the lean gray grimness of Corregidor were there before my eyes in their unchanging cocoon of tropical heat."[69] The general often wrote with the flair and keen eye of a poet.

As the new commander of the Military District of Manila and later of the Philippine Scout Brigade, one of MacArthur's first assignments was to make a thorough study of the Bataan Peninsula and to put together a plan for its defense. He personally surveyed 40 square miles of the malaria-infested promontory, traipsing across "every foot of rugged terrain, over its trails, up and down its steep mountainous slopes, and through its bamboo thickets."[70] MacArthur relished every moment of his fieldwork. Louise was already becoming bored. She missed the glitter and excitement of cities that never slept—Paris, New York, and a panoply of others.

In December 1922, a panel of generals and admirals met in Washington, D.C., and refined an existing strategy for responding to a hypothetical invasion of the Philippines by the Japanese. The strategy was known as War Plan Orange (or WPO). Basically, it called for the defenders to withdraw into the Bataan Peninsula and to fight a delaying action there and on Corregidor Island for six months. This would allow sufficient time, the planners calculated, for a relief expedition to arrive. Some version of War Plan Orange would constitute the only U.S. defense strategy for the Philippines until late 1941. MacArthur did not agree with the plan and would contest it years later.

In February 1923, a cable came from Mary, Arthur III's wife: Pinky was deathly ill and not expected to live.

After World War I, MacArthur reluctantly accepted the responsibility of revamping West Point. It was during this time that he met heiress Louise Cromwell Brooks. He proposed almost immediately and the two were married on St. Valentine's Day, 1922.

Douglas, Louise, and the children sailed at once for home. By the time they arrived in Washington in March, Pinky had nearly recovered. MacArthur and his family turned around and steamed back to Manila. If little else, the trip afforded Douglas a last chance to see his brother: Tragically, Arthur III died prematurely of appendicitis on December 2, 1923. He had by then attained a captain's rank, command of a battleship, and a Navy Cross (second only to the Medal of Honor).

In 1924, Pinky was sufficiently recovered to resume lobbying in Washington in her son's behalf. Brazenly, she wrote to Pershing, pleading with him to elevate her son to major general: "You could give him his promotion by the stroke of your pen."[71] Whether she influenced him is not known. As one of his last acts as chief of staff, however, Black Jack promoted MacArthur to major general,

War Plan Orange

The origins of War Plan Orange — a United States plan for action in the Pacific Theater in the event of a war with Japan — can be traced as far back as the presidency of Theodore "Teddy" Roosevelt (1901–1909). According to Richard Connaughton, in his book *MacArthur and Defeat in the Philippines,* in March 1905, Roosevelt told U.S. Representative J.A.T. Hull, chairman of the House Committee on Military Affairs, "It may be that the Japanese have designs on the Philippines. I hope not. I am inclined to believe not. But I believe we should put our naval and military preparations in such shape that we can hold the Philippines against any foe." In the subsequent War Plan Orange (WPO) of 1907, the United States officially designated Japan as a potential enemy. (Orange represented Japan in the color-coding scheme of U.S. war plans.)

Over the next 30-plus years, War Plan Orange underwent a number of revisions, but its basic premise was carried forward. The plan called for withdrawing U.S.-Filipino forces into the Bataan Peninsula and fighting a defensive action against Japanese invaders for six months until relief arrived. It remained the sole U.S. strategy for the defense of the Philippines until 1941.

MacArthur disagreed with the strategy set forth in WPO and did not feel bound by it when he took command in the Philippines. "Fortunately," he had noted beforehand, as quoted in William Manchester's *American Caesar: Douglas MacArthur 1880-1964,* "the man who is in command at the time will be the man who will determine the main features of [the] campaign. If he is a big man he will pay no more attention to the stereotyped plans that may be filed in the dusty pigeon holes of the War Department than their merit warrants." MacArthur was *the* big man in the Philippines.

effective on January 15, 1925, making him the youngest major general in the army at age 45.

With his promotion came a rapid succession of commands—first, the Twenty-Third Infantry Brigade in the Philippines; then back to the United States to head the IV Corps area in Atlanta; and finally, on to Baltimore to command the III Corps area. Louise owned a magnificent estate in Baltimore called Rainbow Hill, where she entertained the rich and famous. Back in her own element, she was happy again—at least for the present. Professionally, MacArthur was not.

In October of 1925, MacArthur was ordered to serve on the court-martial board of Colonel William "Billy" Mitchell, a childhood friend and an ardent proponent of airpower. MacArthur called the assignment "one of the most distasteful orders I ever received."[72] In campaigning for a separate air force, the outspoken Mitchell had publicly accused the War and Navy departments of incompetence and was charged with insubordination.

As Mitchell's friend as well as an aspirant to the office of army chief of staff, MacArthur faced a delicate balancing act as a member of the court-martial board. He did not want to betray his friend; neither did he want to anger those in the military hierarchy who might block his appointment to chief of staff. Mitchell was convicted and suspended from duty. MacArthur's critics felt that he had been disloyal to his friend.

MacArthur replied, "I did what I could in his behalf and I helped save him from dismissal. That he was wrong in the violence of his language is self-evident; that he was right in his thesis is equally true and inconvertible."[73] Mitchell resigned his commission in 1926 and continued to champion airpower until his death in 1936. Many airmen turned against MacArthur because of his service on Mitchell's court-martial board. Their animus (hostility) would carry over into World War II.

MacArthur's next assignment proved more to his liking. In 1927, he was named president of the American Olympic Committee. He took over a U.S. Olympic team that had been in disarray and molded it into a team that finished first in the 1928 Olympics held in Holland. "Our victorious team returned to New York with the plaudits of the country ringing in our ears."[74] Louise, conspicuously absent, did not share in her spouse's Olympic triumph. The couple had actually begun living apart in 1927, with Louise living in New York and MacArthur remaining at Rainbow Hill in Baltimore.

In the summer of 1928, MacArthur returned to the Philippines—without Louise and the children—this time as commander of the Department of the Philippines, the top military job. The assignment pleased him immensely. It pleased Louise not at all. While MacArthur was renewing acquaintances with Manuel Quezon and other friends in the islands, Louise was filing for divorce in Reno. MacArthur assented to a divorce on "any grounds that will not compromise my honor."[75] Their divorce became final on June 18, 1929, granted on the ridiculous grounds that MacArthur "failed to provide support"[76] for the multimillionaire heiress.

On August 5, 1930, as MacArthur's third tour in the Philippines was winding down, he received a cable from the War Department: "President [Herbert Hoover] has just announced your detail as Chief of Staff to succeed General Summerall [who had been appointed in 1926]."[77] Returning stateside, MacArthur was sworn in as army chief with the temporary rank of general (four stars) on November 21. He moved into the lavish home assigned to the chief of staff, Quarters Number One, at Fort Myer, Virginia, just outside Washington, D.C.

Pinky, who had been living with her son Arthur's widow, Mary, moved in with her youngest son. She was now 78 years old and frail.

MacArthur assumed his new role just as the nation was entering into a period of economic chaos known as the Great Depression. The peacetime army, which had been cut to a puny force of 12,000 officers and 125,000 enlisted men (including 6,000 Filipino Scouts), demanded all of MacArthur's military and political skills to keep it from being reduced even more. During his term as the army's top soldier, he succeeded in preventing the further decimation of the army, but he continually struggled against deep budget cuts in military spending. One of his greatest challenges as chief came in the summer of 1932.

World War I veterans who came to be known as the Bonus Army marched on Washington to demand bonuses that the government had promised to them. Some 12,000 veterans strong, including their families, gathered in tents and shanties near the nation's Capitol to urge support for a bill in Congress that would expedite the promised bonuses. When the bill was defeated, most of the veterans went home, but a few angry veterans mounted an unruly protest in the Anacostia region of Washington. Local authorities were forced to call on federal assistance to restore order.

MacArthur led an army contingent against the protesters, burned their tents and shanties, and forcibly drove them out of the streets. Two of MacArthur's notable subordinates who helped to quell the disturbance were Majors Dwight D. Eisenhower and George S. Patton, Jr.

A shocked American public decried the use of military force against the veterans, and many observers believed that the event contributed to President Hoover's loss to

During the Great Depression, a throng of World War I veterans descended on Washington, D.C., to demand that the government pay them the bonuses that were promised them for their military service. Believing the "Bonus Army" was part of a Communist conspiracy, MacArthur led a contingent against the protesters, burning the tents and shanties they had erected near the Capitol.

Franklin D. Roosevelt in the presidential election in 1932. But both Hoover and MacArthur sincerely believed that the so-called Bonus March was part of a Communist conspiracy. MacArthur insisted, "Had the President not acted when he did, he would have been derelict in his duty."[78]

Although the traditional term for an army chief of staff was four years, President Roosevelt, who took office in January 1933, held MacArthur over for an additional year to ramrod the War Department's fiscal 1936 budget through Congress. The $353-million budget represented a sizable increase and reflected the gathering threat of war in Europe. During MacArthur's extension, the U.S. government instituted certain measures to divest itself of the Philippine Islands.

In the summer of 1935, as his term neared its end, MacArthur began to ponder his next assignment. At age 55—nine years before the army's retirement age of 64—he did not want to step down to a lesser command. But what else was there? he no doubt asked himself. A change in the status of the Philippines provided his answer. Manuel Quezon, president-elect of the about-to-be Philippine commonwealth, arrived in Washington and invited MacArthur to come to the Philippines.

Quezon wanted MacArthur's help in guiding the emerging commonwealth to maturity and in planning its defenses. MacArthur recognized his invitation as an ideal way to finish out his career in the army. Roosevelt quickly approved the idea and named him "military adviser" to the Philippines.

MacArthur reverted to his permanent rank of major general for his fourth tour of duty in the islands. The army awarded him a second Distinguished Service Medal for his work as chief of staff. George R. Brown summed up his accomplishments in the Washington *Herald*: "General MacArthur has saved [the U.S. Army] by putting through Congress the most constructive program for the land defenses since World War I."[79] The general left Washington amid plaudits and pleasant farewells.

"I sailed from San Francisco in the fall of 1935, on the *President Hoover,*" he wrote later, "accompanied by my mother and a small staff."[80] Pinky, at age 83, was frail and ailing. Other members of MacArthur's retinue included the widow Mary MacArthur and Major Dwight D. Eisenhower, who would now serve as the general's chief of staff.

During a ship's party, MacArthur met Jean Marie Faircloth, a lively, unattached woman of 37 from Murfreesboro, Tennessee, with hazel eyes, soft southern charm, and some resemblance to his mother; she was bright, witty, and urbane. Like Louise, Jean had a great deal of money. When Pinky grew sicker on the voyage across the Pacific, Jean helped Mary tend to her. Mary suggested that Jean cut short a planned visit with friends in Shanghai and accompany the MacArthurs to Manila, and Jean did. As for MacArthur and Jean, it was another case of love at first sight.

In the Philippines, the MacArthurs checked into the Manila Hotel. MacArthur realized that his mother was slipping away. On December 2, less than two months after their arrival, Pinky died of cerebral thrombosis, a blood clot in the brain. MacArthur buried her temporarily in a Manila cemetery. He would later bury her next to his father in the Arlington National Cemetery. "Our devoted comradeship of so many years came to an end,"[81] he wrote later. Major Eisenhower noted that her passing "affected the General's spirit for many months."[82]

MacArthur immersed himself in his work. He began implementing a plan that he had conceived in Washington and had developed further aboard ship. His plan was based loosely on the Swiss military establishment and called for building a cadre (core group) of professional soldiers who would train about 40,000 citizen-soldiers a year at some 100 camps throughout the islands. It also provided for a West Point-type of academy to train officers, an air force of 250 planes, and a navy consisting of 50 torpedo patrol (PT) boats.

Always the optimist—as well as the egotist—MacArthur publicly boasted, "By 1946 I will make the islands a Pacific Switzerland that would cost any invader 500,000 men, three years, and more than more than five billion dollars to conquer. . . . These islands must and will be defended. I am here by the Grace of God. This is my destiny."[83]

6

A Debt to Pay

Unquestionably, the Philippines figured prominently in MacArthur's destiny. And from the moment that he met Jean Marie Faircloth, so, too, did she. In 1937, during a short visit to the United States with Manuel Quezon to solicit support for some of their plans for the new commonwealth, MacArthur married Jean. They exchanged vows in a quiet ceremony in the Municipal Building in New York City on April 30. "It was perhaps the smartest thing I have ever done," MacArthur proclaimed later. "She has been my constant friend, sweetheart, and devoted supporter ever since."[84]

Prior to the nuptials, the general had interred Pinky, his former best friend and devoted supporter for so many years, in

The Philippines were to play a major role in General MacArthur's military career. Philippine President-elect Manuel Quezon made MacArthur field marshal of the emerging island nation, a position he retained only by retiring from the military as a four-star general. This retirement, however, would last only until the United States entered World War II.

the Arlington National Cemetery. Following an unproductive visit in Washington (in which Quezon's insistent demands for early Philippine independence by the end of 1938 had angered President Roosevelt), Quezon continued on to tour Europe. The MacArthurs returned to the

Philippines, where they moved into an air-conditioned penthouse atop a new, five-story wing of the Manila Hotel, complete with sweeping views of Manila Bay. They would not see their native land again for 14 years.

Back in the islands, MacArthur began to feel caught in the middle of a widening rift between Roosevelt and Quezon. His position soon became untenable. Roosevelt, who had become concerned about the security of Hawaii, wanted him to return to the United States and take command of both the Hawaiian Islands and the West Coast. But he had promised Quezon, who had appointed him field marshal of the Philippines in June 1936, that he would serve him for his full six-year term as president.

"I settled both problems," MacArthur noted in his memoirs, "by retiring from the army as a four-star general."[85] His 38 years of service ended officially on December 31, 1937. Seven weeks later, on February 21, 1938, he became a father for the first and only time when Jean presented him with a son, Arthur MacArthur IV.

After MacArthur's retirement, the loss of his active status meant that his repeated requests for military matériel for the Philippines no longer carried official weight with the War Department. Moreover, while the Japanese strengthened its hold on Manchuria (which it had invaded in 1932) and moved aggressively into mainland China during the next two years, the Philippine government limited MacArthur's budget to $8 million. This represented about half of what he needed to meet his military goals — but he came very close.

Meanwhile, on September 1, 1939, German dictator Adolf Hitler launched a *Blitzkrieg* (lightning war) against Poland, allegedly to acquire more *Lebensraum* (living space) for the German people. His action ignited World War II, and the greatest, fiercest war in history exploded upon the world scene. The fall of France and the Battle of Britain,

Hitler's aerial onslaught of England, followed in 1940. The threat of Japanese expansionism loomed larger than ever in the Pacific.

In the spring and summer of 1941, Japan, which had entered into a Tripartite (military assistance) Pact with Germany and Italy to form the Axis Powers, seized Hainan Island in the South China Sea and occupied French Indochina (Vietnam). Provoked by Japan's aggression, President Roosevelt froze all Japanese assets in the United States, cut off all trade with Japan, and closed the Panama Canal to Japanese shipping. His actions moved Japan and the United States to the brink of war. After a few weeks of full military alert at U.S. bases in the Pacific without incident, the tension subsided and Japan and the United States entered into extensive diplomatic negotiations to resolve their differences.

As a result of the alert, American militarists reevaluated U.S. military strategy in the event of war against Germany or Japan or both. In mid-1941, they adopted a war plan called Rainbow 5, which had been in the works for several years. The key element of Rainbow 5 gave priority to the defeat of Germany and further stated: "If Japan does enter the war, the military strategy in the Far East will be defensive."[86] In short, the plan meant Europe first, Asia second. This did not bode well for the Philippines.

On July 27, 1941, MacArthur received a cable from U.S. Army Chief of Staff General George C. Marshall. It read, in part: "Headquarters of the United States Army Forces in the Far East [USAFFE] will be established in Manila, Philippine Islands. You are hereby designated as Commanding General, United States Army Forces in the Far East."[87] MacArthur was reinstated as a major general and elevated the following day to lieutenant general.

MacArthur began an eleventh-hour struggle to prepare his meager command to repel an increasingly more imminent

Japanese invasion. Combining optimism, a lot of egotism, and overconfidence in himself and in the ability of his forces, he managed to persuade his superiors to scrap the WPO concept of a defensive stand in Bataan in favor of meeting the enemy head-on at the beaches. Washington stepped up the trickle of arms and war matériel to the islands with a promise of much more.

On November 24, Washington radioed a warning to all Pacific commanders that a "surprise aggressive movement in any direction, including an attack on the Philippines or Guam"[88] was a possibility. Three days later, following the departure of a Japanese expeditionary force from Shanghai, the War Department cabled a "final alert" to MacArthur. The cable noted the apparent termination of negotiations with the Japanese and warned, "Japanese future unpredictable but hostile action possible at any moment."[89]

MacArthur felt that the messages were too vague to warrant any specific actions. Yet he did not ask for a clarification. Furthermore, he had never really believed that the Japanese regarded the soon-to-become-independent Philippines as American territory. He replied, "everything is in readiness for the conduct of a successful defense."[90]

By December 1941, MacArthur's Far East army numbered some 130,000-plus men, including 22,400 U.S. Regulars, 3,000 Philippine Constabulary (national police), and the 107,000-man Philippine Army, which was only partially trained and equipped. The Far East Air Force under Major General Lewis H. Brereton— 277 aircraft, including 36 B-17 Flying Fortresses and 100 P-40 Warhawks—was also available to MacArthur. Admiral Thomas C. Hart's U.S. Asiatic Fleet—a lone heavy cruiser, 2 light cruisers, 13 destroyers, 28 submarines, and a handful of PT boats—represented the only naval support available to MacArthur.

MacArthur expected the main Japanese landings to

come at Lingayen Gulf on the northwest coast of Luzon. In this anticipation, he was right. He further expected to drive the invaders back into the sea with a strong counterattack at the beaches, while negating enemy air support with a B-17 bombing attack against Japanese air bases in Formosa. In the latter two expectancies, he was dead wrong. At sundown on December 7, 1941, Manila time, as MacArthur watched the sun plunge behind the mountains of Cavite from his penthouse, he was about to experience the consequences of his miscalculations.

"At 3:40 on Sunday morning, December 8, 1941, Manila time, a long-distance call from Washington told me of the Japanese attack on Pearl Harbor," MacArthur wrote later, "but no details were given. . . . My first impression was that the Japanese might well have suffered a serious setback."[91] Eight and a half hours later, a Japanese air fleet of 108 twin-engine bombers and 34 fighters from airfields in Formosa darkened the skies over the Clark Field–Iba air base complex north of Manila. In one dark hour, the Japanese planes wiped out half of Brereton's Far East Air Force.

Lieutenant Colonel Warren J. Clear, a member of MacArthur's staff who survived the bombing attack, later noted, "That raid and the simultaneous attack on other airfields near Manila sealed the fate of Luzon and Corregidor."[92] How the American aircraft could have been caught napping and destroyed—despite repeated warnings—has spurred great controversy to this day. In the end, however, the responsibility resides with the USAFFE commander, Douglas MacArthur.

During the next two days, enemy aircraft launched an all-out assault on northern and southern Luzon. They devastated the naval base at Cavite, on the south side of Manila Bay, and demolished everything in their paths— ships, facilities, munitions, and stores. General Brereton moved the remnants of his air force to Mindanao to avoid its total destruction, and the navy ordered most of what was left of the Asiatic Fleet to Java.

At the same time, Japanese ground forces splashed ashore in preliminary landings at Aparri and Vigan in the north and at Legazpi in the south. These landings were feints to divert MacArthur's attention from the anticipated main-force landings at Lingayen Gulf yet to come. MacArthur did not take the bait. To reporters, he explained, "The basic principle in handling my troops is to hold them intact until the enemy commits himself in force."[93] The enemy committed himself in force on December 22.

Starting at 2:00 A.M., Japanese troops of Lieutenant General Masaharu Homma's Fourteenth Army stormed ashore at Lingayen, established three beachheads, and linked up with the Vigan forces. Shortly past noon, they began barreling down Route 3, the cobblestone military highway leading to Manila, driving the half-trained Filipino troops before them. The dependability and gallantry of a few American and Philippine Scout units prevented a total disaster, but Major General Jonathan M. Wainwright's northern Luzon forces were forced to withdraw in five successive moves.

When MacArthur received word that the enemy had landed a second formidable force at Lamon Bay, 60 miles southeast of Manila, a glance at the map told him that Homma was developing a giant pincer movement against him. He needed to react quickly to prevent the claws of a double envelopment maneuver from snapping shut on his forces. On Christmas Day 1941, from his new headquarters on Corregidor Island, he radioed all of his commanders: "WPO is in effect."[94]

MacArthur's reversion to the superseded War Plan Orange meant an immediate withdrawal of his forces into the Bataan Peninsula. In retrospect, most military

BATTLE FOR MANILA

In the weeks that followed the attack on Pearl Harbor, Japanese forces invaded the Philippines, devastating U.S. forces there. American and Filipino troops made a valiant last stand at Bataan and Corregidor. MacArthur's forces, although outnumbered and short on supplies, were able to inflict significant casualties on the Japanese before being forced to surrender.

observers agree that MacArthur should have invoked that defensive strategy immediately upon the outset of hostilities. Although the Americans moved vast stores of ammunition into Bataan during the next week or so, they managed to lay in only about a month's supply of food and very few vital medical supplies. To make matters worse, an influx of some 26,000 civilians crowded into the peninsula, placing an added drain on the already short supplies. MacArthur put everyone on half-rations at once.

By January 6, 1942, four days after the fall of Manila, all of MacArthur's Luzon forces—about 80,000 American and Filipino troops—had retired safely across the unfordable Pampanga River into the Bataan Peninsula, destroying bridges behind them. They had skillfully executed a precisely coordinated withdrawal—but too late to provision themselves sufficiently for a long defensive action. Under such circumstances, the Battle of Bataan began.

MacArthur established his main defense line—known as the Abucay Line—on either side of Mt. Natib in the center of the peninsula at its base. He was determined to hold back the enemy for as long as possible and often exhorted his troops to fight on for "help is on the way from the United States—thousands of troops and hundreds of planes are being dispatched."[95] They were not, of course, because relief forces were not yet available. But MacArthur did not know that at the time. Besides, encouragements of this sort boosted morale immeasurably.

General Homma sent two columns of troops against the Abucay Line, one on either side of Mt. Natib. Despite unexpectedly stiff resistance, Homma's relentless attackers finally forced MacArthur to withdraw his troops to a more easily defended position along the Bagac-Orion Line on January 22. The fallback line stretched from the Pacific to Manila Bay, about 15 miles from the tip of the peninsula.

After MacArthur's troops met and repulsed repeated Japanese attacks along the new line, Homma adopted a new tactic: He sent amphibious forces well behind the battle line on the western coast. American and Filipino rear echelon troops—aided by PT boat harassment and artillery fire from Corregidor—succeeded in driving the enemy back into the sea during two weeks of fierce fighting from January 29 to February 13.

At this point, Homma, who had suffered severe losses, withdrew from the main front to await reinforcements from Japan. MacArthur took advantage of the ensuing lull in the fighting to comply—albeit reluctantly—with President Roosevelt's firm directive to leave for Australia and assume command of all Allied forces in the Southwest Pacific.

On the evening of March 26, Prime Minister John Curtain of Australia hosted a glittering banquet in honor of MacArthur in Canberra. American ambassador to Australia Nelson T. Johnson electrified the audience by announcing that President Roosevelt had awarded the Medal of Honor to MacArthur. The award citation praised his "gallantry and intrepidity above and beyond the call of duty in action," his "heroic conduct," his "calm judgment in each crisis," and his "utter disregard of personal danger under heavy fire and aerial bombardment."[96]

In truth, MacArthur had clearly mishandled the defense of the Philippines and the powers that be in Washington knew it. His award, however, came in one of the darkest hours in American history—Americans needed a hero. Washington also wanted to counter enemy propaganda that was defiling MacArthur as a "coward" and a "deserter" who had "fled his post."[97] In accepting the award that meant so much to him, MacArthur became part of the only father-son combination in U.S. history to receive the medal.

Upon receiving the medal, MacArthur acknowledged that it was "intended not so much for me personally as it is a recognition of the indomitable courage of the gallant army which it was my honor to command."[98]

Bataan fell on April 9. And at midnight on May 6–7, 1942, General Wainwright, reduced to a three-day water supply, agreed to a cease-fire with Homma and called for the surrender of all American forces in the Philippines. In

After reluctantly withdrawing from the Philippines, MacArthur made his way to Australia, where he met with Prime Minister John Curtain (right). President Roosevelt, in an attempt to counter any negative propaganda regarding MacArthur's retreat, awarded the general the Medal of Honor.

Australia, when asked to comment on the fall of Corregidor, MacArthur told the press:

> Corregidor needs no comment from me. It has sounded its
> own story at the mouth of its guns. It has scrolled its own
> epitaph on enemy tablets. But through the bloody haze of
> its last reverberating shot, I shall always see the visions of its
> grim, gaunt, ghostly men, still unafraid.[99]

In his new role as supreme commander, Southwest Pacific, MacArthur would irresistibly influence the course of the war in the Pacific. Contrary to the navy's strategy of bypassing the Philippines and driving directly across the central Pacific toward Japan, MacArthur forced upon the U.S. Joint Chiefs of Staff (JCS) a second strategy dedicated to the reconquest of the Philippines. He owed a debt to the fallen heroes of Bataan—and to the people of the Philippines—and he meant to pay it.

7

Payment in Full

Repayment of his debt to those left behind in the Philippines became MacArthur's grand obsession over the next two and a half years. His appointment as supreme allied commander, Southwest Pacific Area, effectively split command of Pacific operations between MacArthur and Admiral Chester W. Nimitz, who was simultaneously appointed commander in chief, Pacific Ocean Areas. It rankled MacArthur immensely not to have a single command for the entire Pacific. Throughout the war he remained unshakable in his belief that "of all the faulty decisions of the war, perhaps the most inexplicable was not to unify command of the Pacific." [100]

MacArthur believed just as resolutely, of course, that he

Following the U.S. withdrawal from the Philippines, command of the Pacific arena was divided between MacArthur and Admiral Chester Nimitz (right). Although the alliance between these strong-willed leaders was uneasy, their combined efforts allowed U.S. forces to turn the tide of the Pacific campaign.

should have been named as the single top commander in the Pacific. But naval operations chief Admiral Ernest J. King, a crusty but brilliant strategist, vehemently opposed relegating command of his naval vessels and amphibious forces (marines) to an army general. The

Joint Chiefs of Staff therefore orchestrated a compromise: MacArthur's area of command consisted of Australia, New Guinea, the Philippines, Borneo, the Bismarck Archipelago, and much of the Dutch East Indies (Indonesia). Pacific Fleet commander Nimitz assumed the added responsibility for all forces and operations in the rest of the Pacific. With the interservice bickering and dickering out of the way, the Americans began to strike back at Japan.

When MacArthur arrived in Australia in March 1942, the Australian people stood in fear of an imminent Japanese invasion. With most of their fighting men away in North Africa battling Erwin Rommel's *Afrika Korps,* they lacked the men and means to repulse an invader. The Australians embraced MacArthur as the first sign of their salvation. And he rejoiced in their adoration. "I already feel at home,"[101] he told his Canberra audience.

In a voice thick with emotion, he went on to address their concerns. "There can be no compromise. We shall win or we shall die, and to this end I pledge the full resources of all the power of my mighty country and all the blood of my countrymen."[102] His words far exceeded his authority, but they were just what the Australians needed to hear. MacArthur meant his words; in July, he began acting on them.

During May and June, the Japanese extended their perimeter of conquest steadily southward. On July 6, they established a base on Guadalcanal in the Solomon Islands and began building an airfield. Despite their earlier failure to gain control of the Coral Sea in a standoff sea battle with U.S. naval forces (May 7–8), they planned to seize Port Moresby, a key Australian base and the principal city of southern Papua (the southeastern tail of New Guinea). To that end, Japanese forces under the Eighth Army command of Lieutenant General Hitoshi Imamura occupied Gona, on the northeastern coast of Papua, on July 11, and nearby Buna shortly afterward.

Meanwhile, after the resounding U.S. naval victory at Midway (June 4–7), both General MacArthur and Admiral King championed an Allied offensive in the

"Dugout Doug"

Time and again in the course of his 52-year military career, Douglas MacArthur displayed extraordinary leadership and uncommon personal bravery. He exhibited his courage early in his career during skirmishes with guerrilla forces in the Philippines and in Mexico. In World War I, he earned nine decorations for valor under fire and two Purple Hearts for wounds received as a result of enemy action. He emerged from that so-called War to End All Wars as America's most decorated general. Yet, early in World War II, despite his indisputable courage, some of the American defenders of Bataan scathingly mocked him as "Dugout Doug."

In the days immediately following Japan's attack on the Philippines, MacArthur promised his troops that relief from the mighty forces of United States would soon arrive. He did not learn until later that the United States was unprepared to send help. Afterward, probably because of his inability to make good on his promises, he could not bear to face his troops again and thereafter directed the fighting from his headquarters on Corregidor. Mistaking MacArthur's self-imposed isolation for cowardice, his troops composed verses of doggerel sung to the tune of "The Battle Hymn of the Republic." A typical stanza, as quoted in William Manchester's *American Caesar: Douglas MacArthur 1880-1964,* went like this:

Dugout Doug MacArthur lies ashakin' on the Rock
Safe from all the bombers and from any sudden shock
Dugout Doug is eating of the best food on Bataan
And his troops go starving on.

Throughout the Southwest Pacific Area, in Japan and again in Korea, MacArthur repeatedly demonstrated an unquestionable personal bravery that resoundingly repudiated the mythical premise of "Dugout Doug."

Bismarck–New Guinea area to curb the Japanese threat to the U.S.–Australian supply line. King favored a navy-controlled, island-hopping campaign up the Solomons to Rabaul, New Britain, whereas MacArthur argued for an army-controlled, direct thrust on Rabaul itself. The JCS resolved another interservice clash with still another compromise that resulted in the concurrent Papuan (or Buna) and Guadalcanal Campaigns.

The distance across the Papuan Peninsula from Buna in the north to Port Moresby in the south is only 120 miles. Between the two coasts, however, stands the Owen Stanley Mountains, a rugged, jungle-covered range that juts up to heights well over 10,000 feet. The Australians regarded the mountains as impassable. Experienced Japanese jungle fighters under Major General Tomitaro Horii disregarded the Australian opinion. Undeterred by sickness and heavy casualties, they crossed the mountain barrier along the Kokoda Trail and closed to within 32 miles of Port Moresby by mid-September.

When the Australian High Command began considering a withdrawal to the so-called Brisbane Line, which stretched along Australia's heavily populated and industrialized east coast from Brisbane south to Adelaide, MacArthur would have none of it. He told the press, "We must attack, attack, attack!"[103]

MacArthur decided "to make the fight for Australia beyond its own borders. If successful, this would save Australia from invasion and give me an opportunity to pass from defense to offense, to seize the initiative, move forward, and attack."[104] By the end of January 1943, a combined Australian-American force pushed the Japanese back across the Owen Stanleys and took back Buna. And the following month, American marines and soldiers drove the enemy from Guadalcanal. Australians could now breathe easier.

On March 2, U.S. reconnaissance planes sighted a 16-ship convoy steaming west from the Japanese stronghold at Rabaul. With their southward expansion checked, the Japanese were moving to save their troops on New Guinea by reinforcing their garrisons at Lae and Salamaua on the Huon Gulf.

During the four-day aerial onslaught that followed, Major General George C. Kenney's Fifth Air Force, operating from Papua and aided by the Australian Air Force and American PT boats, sank four Japanese destroyers and all of the enemy's eight transports in the Battle of the Bismarck Sea (March 2–5, 1943). Fewer than 1,000 of the 7,000 Japanese reinforcements reached New Guinea. From then on, the Japanese limited traffic in the Bismarck Sea to small, nighttime operations.

Vice Admiral Gunichi Mikawa, commander of the Japanese Eighth Fleet at Rabaul, asserted that the destruction of the convoy "opened the way" for MacArthur's advance to the Philippines and "dealt a fatal blow to the South Pacific operations."[105] A number of his fellow naval officers expressed the same opinion.

By midsummer 1943, MacArthur had four U.S. and six Australian divisions at his disposal and was supported by Vice Admiral William F. "Bull" Halsey's South Pacific fleet. Nimitz, his counterpart in the central Pacific, now commanded nine U.S. army and marine divisions and the Pacific fleet.

For the rest of the year, MacArthur directed a leapfrog campaign along the north coast of New Guinea, while Nimitz executed an island-hopping offensive up the Solomons island chain and westward across the central Pacific. Australian and American troops under Australian General Sir Thomas Blamey occupied Salamaua and Lae in September, and Finschafen, directly across the Solomon Sea from New Britain, fell to the Australian

Ninth Divison on October 2. MacArthur then directed Kenney to attack Rabaul.

Ten days later, according to MacArthur, "Kenney struck like a cobra."[106] Striking with 349 planes, Kenney's Fifth Air Force attacked enemy airstrips, bombed shipping and supply dumps, and left large areas of Rabaul aflame. MacArthur personally cited Kenney later and told him, "George, you broke Rabaul's back yesterday."[107]

Kenney fired back instantly, "The attack marks the turning point in the war in the Southwest Pacific."[108] MacArthur did not hold many aviators in high regard, just as many airmen still resented him because of his part in Billy Mitchell's court-martial. But Kenney was clearly MacArthur's kind of man.

At year's end, elements of MacArthur's First Cavalry Division landed at Arawe, on the southwest coast of New Britain, on December 15. Eleven days later, Nimitz climaxed an island-hopping campaign up the Solomons island chain when the First Marine Division waded ashore at Cape Gloucester in a coordinated move calculated to isolate Rabaul.

"Rabaul was being steadily emasculated," MacArthur noted in his memoirs. "Enemy thrusts from that once-powerful stronghold were becoming weak and ineffectual, and by the end of February 1944 had no air support whatsoever."[109] The tide of battle was indeed turning. Despite Rabaul's isolation, however, the Japanese remained determined to hold their defensive perimeter in western New Guinea. MacArthur was likewise resolved to dislodge them.

Early in 1944, MacArthur supporters in the United States began bandying his name about as a potential candidate for president on the Republican ticket later that year. Publicly, he disavowed any interest in running for the presidency, stating, "I have but one ambition—to return to the

In October 1943, under MacArthur's orders, Major General George C. Kenney initiated a fierce attack on Japanese forces at Rabaul Harbor, sinking several enemy ships, crippling airstrips, and destroying enemy supplies.

Philippines, to save the Philippine people, who are a great people, from their present agony, and to restore the prestige of the United States."[110] But privately, he left little doubt that the notion of becoming president was never far from his mind. For the time being, however, his mind was on returning to the Philippines.

"I was still about 1,600 miles from the Philippines and 2,100 miles from Manila," MacArthur penned later, "but I was now in a position to carry out with increasing speed the massive strokes against the enemy which I had envisioned since the beginning of my campaigns in the Southwest Pacific area."[111] The route that he envisioned lay along the northern coast of New Guinea to the Vogelkop Peninsula and the Moluccas.

From March 30 to April 19, General Kenney's long-range bombers and fighters struck the Japanese airfields at Hollandia, midway along the north coast of New Guinea. Kenney's aircraft shot down some 120 enemy planes in the air and destroyed another 400 on the ground. They eliminated the enemy air threat with only minor losses of their own.

On April 22, before the morning's mists had cleared at Hollandia—the city that had formerly served as the Dutch administrative capital on the island— the Japanese headquarters staff were amazed to see an American invasion force "already in the harbor with their battleships and transports."[112] Two American divisions landed on beaches 25 miles apart, east and west of Hollandia, while two American reinforced regiments hit the shore at Aitape, to the east. Aitape fell to the Americans in two days; Hollandia, in five.

The capture of Hollandia ranks as one of the most brilliant operations of World War II, combining excel-lent planning; skillful coordination of land, sea, and air forces; and near-perfect execution. "The operation throws a loop of envelopment around the [Japanese] Eighteenth Army dispersed along the coast of New Guinea,"[113] MacArthur proclaimed in a triumphant communiqué. He continued his leapfrog campaign west-ward along the New Guinea coast, isolating the Japanese Eighteenth Army and culminating in the capture of Cape Sansapor in July 1944.

MacArthur's offensive converged with that of Admiral Nimitz when his forces landed in Morotai in the Molucca

Islands, between New Guinea and Mindanao in the Philippines, and Nimitz's forces invaded Peleliu in the Palau Islands in September 1944. In seven months, MacArthur's forces had moved forward nearly 1,500 miles, from the Admiralties to Morotai; in ten months, Nimitz's command had advanced more than 4,500 miles, from Hawaii to the Palaus.

Strategy for the next Allied move in the Pacific had been settled in principle the previous month in a conference at Pearl Harbor. General MacArthur and Admiral Nimitz proposed separate concepts for President Roosevelt's consideration. MacArthur wanted to move through the Philippines to Luzon, then on to Japan; Nimitz favored a move against Formosa or the China coast and then on to the Japan. Roosevelt chose MacArthur's plan.

The army and navy staffs then plotted a progressive operation. Their plan called for MacArthur on Mindanao and Nimitz on Yap—225 miles northeast of Palau—to launch a joint assault on Leyte. MacArthur would then move against Luzon, while Nimitz was taking Iwo Jima and Okinawa.

In mid-September, however, based on light enemy air, ground, and naval activity encountered by Bull Halsey's naval forces along the Philippine coast, Nimitz recommended canceling the proposed landings on Mindanao and Yap and instead launching a direct assault against Leyte. MacArthur quickly agreed and boldly advanced his timetable by two months.

On the afternoon of October 20, 1944, MacArthur waded ashore on Leyte with elements of Lieutenant General Walter Krueger's U.S. Sixth Army. In a specially orchestrated event, he spoke into the microphone of a hastily rigged amplifying system and uttered the electrifying words that the Philippine people had waited two and a half years to hear: "People of the Philippines, I have

On October 20, 1944, after U.S. and Australian forces had crippled Japanese naval and air power in the region, MacArthur made good on his promise to return to the Philippines. By December, MacArthur had been promoted to five-star general.

returned."[114] In a moment of high drama, he exhorted them to join him in the fight ahead:

> Rally to me. Let the indomitable spirit of Bataan and Corregidor lead on . . . rise and strike. . . . Strike at every favorable opportunity. For your homes and hearths, strike! For future generations of your sons and daughters, strike! In the name of your sacred dead, strike! Let no heart be faint. Let every arm be steeled.[115]

After his stirring address, MacArthur sat on a fallen tree trunk in a clearing with Philippine President Sergio Osmeña for about an hour in the rain and discussed future relations between the newly restored Philippine government and U.S. forces. (Osmeña had ascended to the presidency upon Manuel Quezon's death earlier that year.) Both men ignored two Japanese planes that swept in low over the beach and dropped their bombs.

After his talk with Osmeña, MacArthur walked toward the recently established command post. When enemy mortar rounds began bursting close by, he noticed his pilot, Major Weldon "Dusty" Rhoades, edging toward the shelter of a tree and asked, "What's the trouble, Dusty, are you worried?"[116] Rhoades confessed that he would feel a bit more at ease with something substantial between himself and the bursting shells.

"Well," MacArthur said, perhaps hoping to comfort him, "the Almighty has given me a job to do and he will see that I am able to finish it."[117]

Rhoades replied that the general's trust in the Almighty was surely a wonderful thing. As for himself, he explained, "I'm just not convinced that God is equally interested in *my* survival."[118] MacArthur strode off, grinning broadly.

In December, MacArthur was promoted to General of the Army with five stars. He expanded the Philippine operation to Mindoro on December 15, 1944, and to Luzon on January 9, 1945. His forces on Luzon recaptured most of the island in a bitter campaign that lasted until Japan surrendered on August 15. In the meantime, his other forces completed the liberation of the Philippines elsewhere and recaptured the coastal oil fields on Borneo.

General of the Army Douglas MacArthur had kept his promise to the courageous defenders of Bataan and Corregidor, and to the people of the Philippines. He had paid his debt to them in full.

8

"Kipling Erred"

On August 15, 1945, the same day on which Japan announced its surrender, U.S. President Harry S Truman, who had become president upon Roosevelt's death in April of that year, appointed MacArthur Supreme Commander for Allied Powers (SCAP) in Japan. Truman ordered him to prepare to accept Japan's formal surrender in Tokyo. MacArthur promptly cabled Truman: "I am deeply grateful for the confidence you have so generously bestowed upon me. . . . I shall do everything possible to capitalize [upon] this situation among the magnificently constructive lines you have conceived for the peace of the world."[119] Thus, the postwar relationship between Truman and MacArthur got off to a friendly start.

Upon the surrender of Japanese forces on August 15, 1945, MacArthur was promoted by President Truman to supreme commander for the Allied powers in Japan. Here, the general arrives at Japan's Atsugi Air Base to begin supervision of the Allied occupation.

MacArthur sent an advance party to Yokohama, Japan's great seaport on Tokyo Bay, to prepare for the formal surrender ceremonies. The party included elements of the U.S. Eleventh Airborne and Twenty-Seventh Infantry Divisions. On August 30, MacArthur and his headquarters staff boarded his C-54 transport named *Bataan* and flew from Manila to the airfield at Atsugi, 40 miles southwest of Tokyo. Five and a half hours later, the general's party touched down at the airfield. MacArthur emerged from his C-54 smoking his corncob pipe and was greeted by Eighth Army commander Lieutenant General Robert L. Eichelberger. They shook hands and MacArthur said, "Bob, from Melbourne to Tokyo is a long way, but this seems to be the end of the road." [120]

The Japanese had provided a string of decrepit vehicles to transport MacArthur's party to the Grand Hotel in Yokohama, 15 miles away, where they would stay until the general made his formal entry into Tokyo. MacArthur ordered his staff to leave their sidearms behind in the plane. General Kenney said later, "It was excellent psychology and made a tremendous impression on the Japanese to see us walking around in their country unarmed . . . To them it meant that there was no doubt about it. They had lost."[121]

Lining the road all the way into Yokohama, a long line of armed Japanese soldiers stood with their backs to MacArthur, supposedly as a symbol of respect. Given the situation, however, the potential for an assassination attempt was not far removed from the minds of MacArthur's retinue, but the general himself seemed unperturbed by such dire possibilities. Kazuo Kawai, a noted Japanese scholar, later captured the moment:

> It was an exhibition of cool personal courage; it was even more a gesture of trust in the good faith of the Japanese. It was a masterpiece of psychology which completely disarmed Japanese apprehensions. From that moment, whatever danger there might have been of a fanatic attack on the Americans vanished in a wave of Japanese admiration and gratitude.[122]

MacArthur's acute understanding of the Eastern mind, developed over long years in Asia, eminently qualified him for the difficult task ahead and would serve him well.

That evening, while MacArthur was dining at his hotel, an aide announced to him that he had a visitor outside: Lieutenant General Jonathan M. Wainwright. He had been flown in from a Japanese prison camp in Mukden (now Shenyang) in northeast China. "I rose and started for the lobby, but before I could reach it, the door swung open and there was Wainwright," MacArthur noted later. "He was haggard and aged. . . . He walked with difficulty and with the help of a cane."[123] The two old soldiers embraced in an emotional reunion. Wainwright, for resisting Japanese efforts to break his spirits during almost four years of captivity, received the Medal of Honor.

MacArthur accepted Japan's formal surrender aboard the U.S. battleship *Missouri* in Tokyo Bay on September 2, 1945. By 9:25 A.M., everyone, including Admiral Nimitz, had signed the surrender document. MacArthur rose from the table beneath the *Missouri*'s 16-inch guns and said, "Let us pray that peace be now restored to the world and that God will preserve it always. These proceedings are now closed."[124]

After the Japanese surrender, MacArthur also assumed command of the Allied Occupation Forces in Japan. For almost six years, he served as a virtual viceroy—a governor of a country or province who rules as the representative of a king or sovereign. During this time, he directed the reorganization and reconstruction of the governmental, social, and economic systems of Japan.

On September 3, to set the machinery of the occupation in motion, MacArthur issued three proclamations. One announced the installation of a military-type government and invoked English as its official language. The second introduced a military-court system with harsh punishments, including the death penalty, for occupation resisters. A third proclaimed scrip—that is, military currency—as the legal tender of the land.

On September 8, MacArthur moved into the newly renovated American Embassy where he would reside with Jean, Arthur IV, and his household staff throughout the occupation. As SCAP headquarters, he selected a six-story building in downtown Tokyo that had once housed a large insurance firm. From his office on the sixth floor of the Dai Ichi (Number One) Building, as it became known, MacArthur could look across the moat surrounding Emperor Hirohito's palace.

One can only wonder how many times MacArthur must have stared toward that partially burned-out palace and pondered the enormity of his task as SCAP. "I, a professional soldier," he wrote later, "had the civil responsibility and absolute control over almost 80 million people, and I would maintain that control until Japan had once more demonstrated that it was ready, willing, and

War Crimes Trials

In postwar Japan, an International Military Tribunal for the Far East convened in Tokyo to prosecute Japanese war criminals charged with crimes against peace, crimes against humanity, murder, and atrocities. With these trials, the Allies hoped to accomplish two things: to punish those responsible for starting the war or condoning or committing atrocities, and to send the message to the Japanese people that there is a price to pay for waging war. These trials dragged on until November 1948.

The trials were categorized in three classes of war criminal: Twenty-five of the "A" criminals, such as Hideki Tojo, Japan's prime minister, were tried by the Military Tribunal in Tokyo. Six generals and one civilian were hanged, 16 received life sentences, and two got lesser sentences.

Twenty-odd high-ranking generals whose troops had committed atrocities made up the "B" offenders. Military courts established by MacArthur's command (SCAP) tried them. Two (including General Masaharu Homma, who was blamed for the Bataan Death March) were executed. All others were acquitted.

The "C" criminals numbered some 4,200 who were charged with minor atrocities or mistreatment of prisoners of war. (This class included Tokyo Rose, the American-born propagandist). Various Allied military courts tried them. About 700 were executed, some 400 were acquitted, and the rest were imprisoned for varying sentences.

able to become a responsible member of the family of free nations."[125] Great moments in time invariably spawn great leaders to match the moment. As the director of Japan's postwar rehabilitation, Douglas MacArthur was undeniably the right man in the right place at the right time.

"From the moment of my appointment as supreme commander," MacArthur noted later, "I had formulated the policies I intended to follow, implementing them through the emperor and the machinery of the imperial government. I was thoroughly familiar with the Japanese administration, its weaknesses and its strengths, and felt the reforms I contemplated were those which would bring Japan abreast of modern progressive thought and action."[126] In his memoirs, he outlined his agenda:

> First destroy the military power. Punish war criminals. Build the structure of representative government. Modernize the constitution. Hold free elections. Enfranchise the women. Release the political prisoners. Liberate the farmers. Establish a free labor movement. Encourage a free economy. Abolish police oppression. Develop a free and responsible press. Liberalize education. Decentralize the political power. Separate church from state.[127]

In little more than half a decade, MacArthur accomplished all these things—some with ease, others with great difficulty. He began by demobilizing nearly 7 million men of Japan's armed services, releasing political prisoners and prisoners of war, decentralizing the hated national police, and prosecuting war criminals in trials that dragged on until November 1948. Over the strong objections of the Australians and others, MacArthur refused to prosecute Emperor Hirohito as a war criminal. And when rumors suggested that Hirohito planned to abdicate as a way of

Although MacArthur presided at the Japanese surrender, ending World War II, he refused to try Japan's Emperor Hirohito (right) as a war criminal, insisting instead that the emperor retain his post as a "matter of duty."

atoning for his role in the war, MacArthur insisted that he stay "as a matter of duty."[128]

Japanese foreign minister Shigeru Yoshida concluded that MacArthur's respectful treatment of the emperor — his order that "every honor due a sovereign is to be his" and his refusal to try and execute Hirohito for war crimes—"more than any other single factor made the occupation an historic success."[129]

Another of the first things MacArthur did was to banish Shinto as the state religion. The Shinto religion held that the emperor was descended from the sun goddess and as such was divine. The emperor was encouraged to travel about the land visiting sporting events, concerts, and other public activities in the manner of European sovereigns. In this way, he became like a conventional monarch. Hirohito renounced his divinity on January 1, 1946, probably at the encouragement of MacArthur.

In 1946, MacArthur initiated a purge program, abolishing Japan's ultranationalist, militarist, and feudal beliefs and systems, replacing them with more liberal and democratic ideologies. Unlike the "de-Nazification" program in Germany, the purge was carried out "with as little harshness as possible."[130] Though not entirely effective, it broke the hold of the old-line militarists, industrialists, and politicians and enabled fresh leaders to emerge.

In March, MacArthur and Japanese officials introduced a liberal constitution and reformed Japan's political system. The new constitution reduced the emperor to the status of a "symbol" of Japan. It also created a three-part government like that of the United States with a legislative, judicial, and executive branch. It contained the famous no-war clause: "The people forever renounce war as a sovereign right of the Nation and the threat or use of force as a means of settling international disputes."[131] Beyond a moderate self-defense force, there would never again be a Japanese army, navy, or air force. The new body of laws was placed before the Japanese people for a vote in the first general election—in which women voted for the first time—in April 1946. The people approved it with an overwhelming vote, and it became the law of the land in May 1947.

Five months earlier, as though MacArthur lacked for something to do, President Truman appointed him commander of the Far East Command in January 1947. His additional command encompassed all U.S. forces in Japan, the Ryukyus, the Philippines, the Marianas, the Bonin Islands, and Korea. Seldom, if ever, has an American military officer borne such enormous responsibility and wielded such awesome authority. Lesser men might have buckled under the weight of such demands. MacArthur, at 67, thrived on the increased responsibility and grew stronger.

The reform of Japan's economy posed the greatest challenge to MacArthur, but he eventually established a new competitive enterprise with a broader-based ownership that afforded workers a larger share of the profits. He loosened the grip of the *Zaibatsu*, huge industrial combines that had once dominated the economy. Under the new constitution, all people—both male and female—had "the right and obligation" to work, and "the right of workers to organize and to bargain and act collectively"[132] was guaranteed.

Along with labor reform, MacArthur instituted land reforms. The Diet—Japan's national law-making body—passed sweeping legislation designed to correct the inequities and slave-like conditions imposed by many dictatorial landlords. One key law directed the Japanese government to purchase some 5 million acres of farmland and then resell it to the tenants on long-term loans. As a result, by 1950, free, independent farmers owned and worked 89 percent of Japan's arable land. MacArthur characterized the program as "the most successful experiment of its kind in history."[133]

One by one, MacArthur met his stated goals—changing

outmoded social norms, modernizing the health and welfare programs and the educational system, establishing a free press, redistributing political power from Tokyo to the local scene, and instituting a wealth of other Western-style innovations. Many of his changes helped to promote better relations between the United States and Japan.

Rudyard Kipling, the distinguished British author and poet, once wrote: "Oh, East is East, and West is West, and never the twain [two] shall meet." [134] Notwithstanding the poet's surmise, in *The Ballad of East and West*, the people of Japan took MacArthur to their hearts. They readily adapted to his innovations and showed a remarkable ability to embrace Western ideas, methods, style, and conventions, just as they had after the Meiji reforms. (The Meiji period from 1868 to 1912 signifies Japan's emergence into the modern era.) In less than a decade of occupation, with American GIs (servicemen) as ambassadors of the American way, the Japanese people became demilitarized, democratized, and — with an unsurpassed passion for baseball, pop music, and Hollywood films — *Americanized*.

General Courtney Whitney, who headed the Government Section in Tokyo during the Occupation, said it right: "Kipling erred; the twain *did* meet." [135]

Going Home

Early in the morning of Sunday, June 25, 1950—well into the fifth year of Japan's occupation and westernization—the telephone rang in MacArthur's bedroom at the American Embassy in Tokyo. MacArthur picked up the phone with a sense of urgency. It was the duty officer at his headquarters in the Dai Ichi Building. "General," he said, "we have just received a dispatch from Seoul [the capital of South Korea], advising that the North Koreans have struck in great strength south across the 38th Parallel at four o'clock this morning." [136]

MacArthur's first thought was of another telephone call that had awakened him in his penthouse atop the Manila Hotel almost a decade earlier. That call too had come early on a

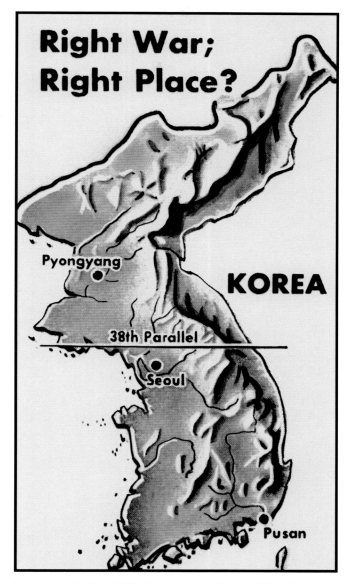

**Right War;
Right Place?**

Pyongyang

KOREA

38th Parallel

Seoul

Pusan

Even though World War II was over, General MacArthur's military career was not yet at its end. When North Korean forces crossed the 38th parallel into South Korea in June 1950, President Truman ordered MacArthur to provide support for South Korean forces. Within a month, MacArthur was named supreme commander of United Nations forces in Korea.

Sunday morning. "It was the same fell note of the war cry that was again ringing in my ears," he wrote later. "It couldn't be, I told myself. Not again!"[137] But thousands of communist North Korean troops had already poured across the frontier into South Korea, moving southward and sweeping aside opposition with the speed and force of rampaging waters from a ruptured dam. And the war cry that rang again in MacArthur's ears was one last call to arms. The Korean War (1950–1953) had begun.

In a narrow sense, the communist incursion marked the beginning of a civil war between peoples of a divided nation; in a broader sense, it signified the heating up of the Cold War and the outbreak of open hostilities between communist and free-world factions. President Harry S Truman, who had been spending the weekend at his home in Independence, Missouri, flew back to Washington as soon as he heard the news of North Korea's aggression. He had already begun to consider U.S. intervention on South Korea's behalf. "If the communists were permitted to force their way into the Republic of South Korea without opposition from the free world," he wrote later, "no small nation would have the courage to resist threats and aggression by stronger communist neighbors."[138]

On June 27, President Truman authorized General MacArthur to provide U.S. air and naval support to the South Koreans. In quick succession, he ordered the blockade and bombing of North Korea. Two days later, MacArthur flew to Suwon, south of Seoul, to observe the action up close. In a cable to Washington on June 30, he recommended "the introduction of U.S. ground combat forces into the Korean battle area."[139] The president authorized the use of one regimental combat team as a stopgap measure pending a further buildup of American ground troops. America was at war again.

On July 7, the United Nations (UN) asked the United States to act as its executive agent in organizing a United Nations Command for prosecuting the Korean War. Truman accepted the responsibility and the next day named MacArthur as supreme commander of UN Forces in Korea. Upon MacArthur's appointment, an editorial of *The New York Times* proclaimed, in part: "In every home in the United States today there must be a sure conviction that if any man can carry out successfully the task which Truman and the Security Council of the United Nations have given him, and carry out the task honorably, efficiently and with no waste of life and effort, that man is the good soldier in Tokyo who has long since proved to the hilt his ability to serve his country well."[140] In the tough days ahead, the general would need every ounce of his ability to stave off defeat.

The forces of North Korean Premier Kim Il Sung — 135,000 strong — consisted of 8 full divisions, each containing a regiment of artillery; 2 half-strength divisions, 2 separate regiments; an armored brigade with 120 Soviet T34 medium tanks; and 5 border constabulary brigades. Kim could also call on 180 Soviet aircraft, mostly fighters and bombers, and a few naval patrol craft.

By contrast, the smaller Republic of (South) Korea Army, popularly known as the ROKs, numbered only 95,000 half-trained troops. Of its 8 divisions, only 4 approached full strength. The ROKs had no tanks and only 89 105-mm howitzers (short cannon with high trajectories). Although the ROK Navy matched its North Korean counterpart, the ROK Air Force consisted of only a few trainers and liaison aircraft. Even with their rapidly deteriorating U.S.-supplied equipment, the South Koreans possessed only enough supplies on hand to sustain combat operations for about 15 days.

Still worse, from the standpoint of South Korea and

the United Nations, the once-mighty wartime strength of the United States, as MacArthur put it, "had been frittered away in a bankruptcy of positive and courageous [U.S.] leadership toward any long-range objectives."[141] In short, neither the Republic of Korea nor the United Nations was capable of stopping the North Koreans during the first three months of the Korean conflict. As a result, the speed of the initial North Korean attack, combined with the unpreparedness of the ROK troops, enabled the North Korean Peoples Army (NKPA) to overrun most of the peninsula before U.S. forces could reach the battleground.

Even when the UN forces arrived—made up mostly of the U.S. Eighth Army, which had been serving on occupation duty in Japan—the NKPA virtually surrounded them and reduced MacArthur's forces to a defensive perimeter around the port of Pusan in southeast Korea. MacArthur halted the North Korean drive along the Naktong River, then directed the defense of what came to be known as the Pusan (or Naktong) Perimeter. For a time, it must have seemed like Bataan all over again to the 70-year-old general. But this time MacArthur moved with stunning swiftness into his finest hour as a soldier.

MacArthur's grand strategy for an amphibious envelopment of the NKPA forces attacking the Pusan Perimeter— a watery end run of sorts—had probably started stirring in his mind during his front-line visit to Suwon. His plan for Operation Chromite—the code name for the Inchon invasion—basically called for an amphibious force to land at Inchon, on the west coast of Korea, behind the NKPA forces. This force would then serve as an anvil against which the U.S. Eighth Army defending Pusan could hammer the North Koreans in a simultaneous breakout from the perimeter and northward drive.

MacArthur met strong resistance to his plan, mainly for two reasons: Enemy defensive strength at Inchon was largely indiscernible, and the treacherous tides at Inchon posed a great risk for any naval and amphibious forces. Over the qualms and objections of the Joint Chiefs of Staff and other critics, MacArthur formed the U.S. X (Tenth) Corps. It consisted of the U.S. Seventh Infantry Division and the First Marine Division. In late August, MacArthur addressed the doubts of the JCS:

> The very arguments you have made as to the impracticalities involved will tend to ensure the element of surprise. For the enemy commander will reason that no one would be so brash as to make such an attempt. . . . I can almost hear the ticking of the second hand of destiny. We must act now or we will die. . . . We shall land at Inchon, and I shall crush them.[142]

On September 15, the First Marine Division landed at Inchon, followed by the Seventh Infantry Division, and proceeded to turn MacArthur's prediction into reality. In a brilliant amphibious envelopment maneuver, the marines recaptured Seoul on September 27.

Meanwhile, a day earlier, lead elements of the Seventh Cavalry Regiment, First Cavalry Division, had linked up with elements of the 31st Infantry Regiment, Seventh Infantry Division, near Osan. The hammer had met the anvil. The UN forces had virtually destroyed the North Korean People's Army. Except for a scattering of guerrillas left behind, the remnants of the North Korean People's Army fled back across the 38th parallel. The hugely successful Inchon campaign will always stand out as MacArthur's military masterpiece.

On September 29, with a dramatic speech delivered in his characteristically grand manner, MacArthur

In a bold move, MacArthur saw the weakness of the North Korean People's
Army at Inchon and ordered a combined land and amphibious attack that,
although controversial, proved overwhelmingly successful. Here, the
general leans on the barrel of an enemy tank as he inspects the extent of
the allied attack at Inchon.

returned Seoul to South Korean President Syngman Rhee.
"And, when the ceremony was over," the general wrote
later, "the people of Seoul lined the streets and clapped
and waved their little paper flags. I returned to
Tokyo."[143] The original war aims of UN forces in
Korea—that is, the restoration of the preinvasion status
quo—had been achieved, and much of the world felt
that the Korean conflict had ended.

That same day, however, MacArthur received a
"for-his-eyes-only" message from the (now) Secretary of
Defense George C. Marshall. Its key part stated: "We want
you to feel unhampered tactically and strategically to proceed
north of the 38th parallel."[144] The crux of Marshall's
carefully worded message supported a general feeling in the
United Nations that the war would not be truly over until

the NKPA was totally destroyed. The message hinted that should MacArthur find it militarily necessary to move across the 38th parallel, the United Nations would prefer to learn about it after the fact so as to make a formal UN response—either pro or con—unnecessary.

Replying on September 30, MacArthur said that "parallel 38 is not a factor in the military employment of our forces," and that "I regard all of Korea open for our military operations."[145] MacArthur went on to say that he intended to make his views public. That was precisely what Marshall wanted to avoid—and with good reason.

Beginning in August 1950, Communist China—which looked upon communist North Korea as a buffer state between itself and the democratic Republic of Korea—had already begun denouncing UN actions in Korea in a series of drumbeat admonitions. On October 1, Red China's Premier Zhou Enlai declared that the Chinese people "absolutely will not tolerate foreign aggression, nor will they supinely tolerate seeing their neighbors being savagely invaded by the imperialists."[146]

On October 7, despite the diplomatic delicacy of the situation, the United Nations General Assembly passed a resolution authorizing the use of UN troops anywhere north of the 38th parallel to establish a unified and democratic Korea. MacArthur accepted the resolution as a mandate to liberate North Korea from communist control. Two days later, after having ascended to the pinnacle of his career, he committed one of the cardinal sins of a military leader: He split his forces in the face of an enemy. MacArthur's long military career then turned precipitously downward.

MacArthur first ordered the Eighth Army to advance to the North Korean capital of Pyongyang and then to continue north to the Manchurian frontier at the Yalu River. He then sent X Corps off to the east coast of Korea and directed it to drive northward, also to the Yalu.

MacArthur ignored the mountainous terrain between his two forces.

On October 15, a confident MacArthur flew to Wake Island for a one-day conference about the Korean situation with President Truman. MacArthur optimistically predicted the end of organized enemy resistance by Thanksgiving. He further foretold the return of the Eighth Army to Japan by Christmas. When the president asked him about the chances of Chinese intervention, MacArthur replied, "Very little."[147] He was wrong.

During the rest of October and most of November, MacArthur's twin drives northward worked well against the fleeing remnants of the NKPA. But late in November, the Chinese intervened and moved massive forces into the unguarded mountainous region. The 130,000-man Thirteenth Army Group of the massed Chinese Communist Forces (CCF) struck the Eighth Army front in the west, and the CCF 120,000-man Ninth Army Group assaulted X Corps at the Chosin Reservoir in the east. The numerically superior CCF forces quickly forced MacArthur's divided forces to retreat south of the 38th parallel. MacArthur skillfully directed a fighting withdrawal and managed to stabilize the front south of Seoul by March 1951.

With China's intervention, MacArthur saw the Korean conflict as a whole new war and advocated the bombing of bases in China. The president and his advisers, feeling that striking the Chinese mainland might lead to a larger war, denied MacArthur's recommendation. On March 6, MacArthur called a press conference in which he deplored "our existing conditions of restraint."[148] Speaking beyond his authority, he predicted that, unless the Pentagon supplied "major additions" to the Eighth Army, the battle lines in the end would reach a "point of theoretical stalemate."[149] His troops regained Seoul on March 14 and again drove into North Korea.

On March 20, the Joint Chiefs of Staff informed MacArthur that the president and members of the State and Defense departments were preparing a statement that the UN would consider negotiating peace terms with China. Basically, the Truman administration had changed its national policy from a strategic aim of *rolling back* communism to one of *containing* communism. Since Truman had already issued a directive ordering all government and military officials to refrain from public statements on foreign policy without clearance, no one expected that MacArthur would do anything to interfere with a peace-making attempt. But MacArthur felt that he had the enemy on the run and again spoke out of turn.

On March 26, MacArthur issued a statement to the press that reflected his own counterpolicy of expanding the war. It said, in part: "The enemy . . . must by now be painfully aware that a decision of the United Nations to depart from its tolerant effort to contain the war to the area of Korea through expansion of our military operations to his coastal areas and interior bases would doom Red China to the risk of imminent military collapse."[150] His statement was saber rattling at its best and publicly contravened the new policy of his commander in chief, Harry S Truman.

Three days later, on March 29, Peiping (Beijing) Radio rejected MacArthur's statement as an "insult to the Chinese people" and "nothing but a demand for the Chinese and Korean forces to yield to the so-called United Nations forces, [as well as] a threat that the aggressors will advance on our homeland."[151]

President Truman was furious and later wrote, "By this act MacArthur left me no choice—I could no longer tolerate his insubordination."[152] But he did not act at once.

In the meantime, on April 5, U.S. congressman Joseph W. Martin, an advocate for winning the war in Korea, read a letter from MacArthur on the floor of the U.S. House of

On April 11, 1951, President Truman recalled MacArthur from the Pacific and stripped him of his title as supreme commander. A week later, he and his wife, Jean, returned to the United States for the first time in 14 years. Here, Jean MacArthur is offered an autograph book to sign by an admirer.

Representatives. Martin had written to him for his views on Truman's limited-war policy. MacArthur concluded his response this way:

> It seems strangely difficult for some to realize that here in Asia is where the Communist conspirators have elected to make their play for global conquest, and that we have joined the issue thus raised on the battlefield; that here we fight Europe's war with arms, while the diplomats there still fight it with words; that if we lost the war to Communism in Asia the fall of Europe is inevitable; win it, and Europe most probably would avoid war and yet preserve freedom. As you point out, we must win. There is no substitute for victory.[153]

On April 11, 1951, 71-year-old General of the Army Douglas MacArthur received the following message from President Truman:

> I deeply regret that it becomes my duty as President and Commander in Chief of the United States military forces to replace you as Supreme Commander, Allied Powers; Commander in Chief, United Nations command; Commander in Chief, Far East; and Commanding General, U.S. Army, Far East.[154]

A few minutes earlier, the news had reached MacArthur in Tokyo via a radio broadcast while he was entertaining luncheon guests. He received the public humiliation without a trace of emotion showing on his face. He turned in his chair and looked up at his wife, who was standing behind him with her hand on his shoulder. "Jeannie," he said gently, "we're going home at last."[155]

Afterword: Echoes

After 14 long, dramatically historic years in Asia, the MacArthurs—Douglas, Jean, Arthur IV, and their small party, including the ever-faithful Ah Cheu—boarded the *Bataan* for the flight home at the airfield in Atsugi. They had said fond farewells to a host of well-wishers, from Emperor Hirohito down through the military and diplomatic chain of command. An army band struck up *Auld Lang Syne* and army cannon thundered a 19-gun salute as the general's plane roared down the runway, lifted into the air, and disappeared into the vast grayness of an early morning April sky.

Across the Sea of Japan to the west, the general left behind him a political war that was fated to rage on for more than two more bloody years, while negotiators on both sides haggled, primarily, over the postwar status of prisoners of war.

MacArthur received a hero's welcome during a stopover in San Francisco. "Our welcome home was tumultuous," he wrote later. "It seemed to me that every man, woman, and child in San Francisco turned out to cheer us."[156] The *Bataan* flew on to its final destination in Washington, D.C., where another huge turnout of admirers welcomed him home.

On April 19, 1951, he delivered his farewell address to a joint session of Congress and the nation, in which he reviewed the conditions in Asia and his aggressive policies for dealing with them. His now-famous conclusion, which consigned a lifetime of service to history, evoked tears from millions of his countrymen:

> I am closing my fifty-two years of military service. When I joined the army even before the turn of the century, it was the fulfillment of all my boyish hopes and dreams. The world has turned over many times since I took the oath on the Plain at West Point, and the hopes and dreams have long since vanished. But I still remember the refrain of one of the most popular barrack ballads of that day which proclaimed most proudly that—
>
> "Old soldiers never die, they just fade away."
>
> And like the old soldier of that ballad, I now close my military career and just fade away—an old soldier who tried to do his duty as God gave him the light to see that duty.
>
> Good-by.[157]

He spoke his last word in a barely audible hush.

MacArthur did not instantly fade away. For the next two months, he appeared before a congressional hearing, trying to convince Congress that an all-out stand against communism was needed not only in Asia but also around the world. His efforts failed and the policies of the Truman administration prevailed. President Truman could have brought charges against MacArthur but he did not. MacArthur had never directly disobeyed an order, but the general had clearly undermined administration policies in Korea. Truman, however, deemed MacArthur's dismissal as punishment enough.

For the next decade, MacArthur remained active, giving speeches, serving as the chairman of the board of Remington Rand (later Sperry Rand), and writing his memoirs, *Reminiscences*, while residing in New York City at the Waldorf Astoria Hotel.

In May 1962, a now ailing General of the Army Douglas MacArthur (Retired) traveled to West Point to receive the coveted Sylvanus Thayer Award for distinguished service to the nation. In accepting the Military Academy's highest accolade, MacArthur said, in part:

> In my dreams I hear again the crash of guns, the rattle of musketry, the strange mournful mutter of the battlefield. But in the evening of my memory, always I come back to West Point. Always there echoes and reechoes— Duty-Honor-Country.[158]

In return for the tribute from the Corps of Cadets, he left the future officers with three words to live their lives by as he had lived his own; three words that by themselves define the man and the sum of his existence: Duty, Honor, Country. Long may they echo on the Plain at West Point.

TAPS

On April 5, 1964, the general died in Walter Reed Medical Center in Washington, D.C., from acute liver and kidney failure after a gradual wasting away. He was 84. President Lyndon B. Johnson accorded him the funeral that he deserved, and he was interred in a magnificent marble memorial within the former city hall in Norfolk, Virginia.

MacArthur was a great paradox of a man, equally brilliant and controversial. A superb strategist—witness Hollandia and Inchon—he was egotistical and arrogant to a fault. But he was also a man of great compassion for those who served under him, for his fellow Americans, and for the people of the Philippines and Japan. Arguably, no man ever loved his country more or served it better. As long as a single battle remains to be fought, the name and deeds of General of the Army Douglas MacArthur will reverberate from the pantheon of great American generals . . . like a trumpet's call to arms.

1880

January 26   Douglas MacArthur is born in Little Rock Barracks, Arkansas.

1893   Enters West Texas Military Academy in San Antonio, Texas.

1897   Graduates from West Texas Military Academy at the top of his class.

1899   Enters U.S. Military Academy at West Point, New York.

1903   Graduates from U.S. Military Academy as first captain and first in class; as a second lieutenant, he is assigned to the Corps of Engineers and sent to the Philippines, where he comes under fire for the first time.

1904   Promoted to first lieutenant.

1905   Tours Far East with his parents, Arthur MacArthur Jr. and Mary Pinkney "Pinky" Hardy MacArthur.

1906   Appointed aide to President Theodore Roosevelt.

1911   Promoted to captain.

1912   Arthur MacArthur Jr. dies.

1913   Appointed to general staff.

1914   Recommended for Medal of Honor for daring escapade in Vera Cruz.

1915   Promoted to major.

1917   As a colonel, serves as chief of staff of the Rainbow Division.

1918   Decorated nine times while fighting in France; becomes a general at age 38; commands the Rainbow Division.

1919   Appointed superintendent of West Point.

1922   On February 14, weds Henriette Louise Cromwell Brooks.

1925   Serves on court-martial of Billy Mitchell.

1930   Becomes Army Chief of Staff at age 50.

1932   Leads an army contingent against Bonus Army protesters.

1935   Pinky dies in Manila.

1936   Appointed Philippine field marshal.

1937   Weds Jean Marie Faircloth.

1938   Retires from the U.S. Army; Arthur MacArthur IV is born in Manila.

1941   Recalled to active duty by President Franklin D. Roosevelt and appointed U.S. Far East commander; Japanese attack Pearl Harbor and the Philippines; U.S.–Filipino forces defend Bataan and Corregidor.

1942	Escapes from the Philippines with family; awarded the Medal of Honor in Australia; appointed Supreme Allied Commander, Southwest Pacific Area; begins campaign in New Guinea.
1943	Bypasses Rabaul.
1944	Directs capture of Hollandia, a masterpiece of strategy; promoted to General of the Army.
1945	Returns to the Philippines and recaptures Manila, Bataan, Corregidor, and liberates the islands from Japanese control; accepts Japan's surrender; assumes command of Allied occupation forces in Japan and directs Japan's recovery in the postwar world.
1950	Named commander of UN forces as Korean War begins; devises and directs the invasion at Inchon, his crowning military achievement; Chinese enter the war.
1951	Undermines Truman's peace plans and is relieved of all commands.
1962	Bids farewell to West Point.
1964	Douglas MacArthur dies at Walter Reed Medical Center in Washington, D.C., and is entombed in Norfolk, Virginia.

CHAPTER 1

1. Quoted in Clay Blair Jr., *MacArthur*. Garden City, NY: Doubleday, 1977, p. 71.
2. Quoted in Richard Connaughton, *MacArthur and Defeat in the Philippines*. Woodstock, NY: The Overlook Press, 2001, p. 281.
3. Quoted in Geoffrey Perret, *Old Soldiers Never Die: The Life of Douglas MacArthur*. Holbrook, MA: Adams Media, 1996, p. 273.
4. Quoted in William Manchester, *American Caesar: Douglas MacArthur 1880–1964*. Boston: Little, Brown, 1978, p. 253.
5. Quoted in Louis Morton, *The Fall of the Philippines*. United States Army in World War II: The War in the Pacific. Minnetonka, MN: National Historical Society, 1995, p. 357.
6. Ibid., pp. 357–58.
7. Quoted in John Toland, *But Not in Shame: The Six Months after Pearl Harbor*. New York: Signet Books, 1962, p. 294.
8. Quoted in John Costello, *The Pacific War 1941–1945*. New York: Quill, 1982, p. 213.
9. Quoted in Perret, *Old Soldiers Never Die*, p. 274.
10. Quoted in Toland, *But Not in Shame*, p. 295.
11. Ibid.
12. Douglas MacArthur, *Reminiscenses: General of the Army Douglas MacArthur*. Annapolis, MD: Naval Institute Press, 2001, p. 142.
13. Quoted in Manchester, *American Caesar*, p. 257.
14. Quoted in Blair, *MacArthur*, p. 74.
15. Quoted in Manchester, *American Caesar*, p. 259.
16. Ibid., p. 261.
17. Ibid.
18. Ibid., p. 263.
19. Quoted in Blair, *MacArthur*, p. 76.
20. Ibid., pp. 76–77.

CHAPTER 2

21. Quoted in Manchester, *American Caesar*, p. 14.
22. Ibid., p. 15.
23. Quoted in Trevor N. Dupuy, Curt Johnson, and David L. Bongard, *The Harper Encyclopedia of Military Biography*. New York: HarperCollins, 1992, p. 461.
24. Quoted in Manchester, *American Caesar*, p. 20.
25. Quoted in Perret, *Old Soldiers Never Die*, p. 11.
26. Quoted in Blair, *MacArthur*, pp. 7–8.
27. Ibid., p. 8.
28. MacArthur, *Reminiscenses*, p. 16.
29. Ibid., p. 17.
30. Ibid., p. 18.
31. Quoted in Manchester, *American Caesar*, p. 47.
32. Ibid.
33. Quoted in Manchester, *American Caesar*, p. 50.
34. Ibid., p. 29.
35. Quoted in Blair, *MacArthur*, p. 12.
36. Quoted in Perret, *Old Soldiers Never Die,* p. 49.

CHAPTER 3

37. Quoted in Manchester, *American Caesar,* p. 64.
38. MacArthur, *Reminiscenses,* p. 30.
39. Quoted in Blair, *MacArthur,* p. 12.
40. Ibid.
41. Ibid., p. 13.
42. Ibid.
43. MacArthur, *Reminiscenses,* p. 33.
44. Ibid., p. 40.
45. Ibid., p. 42.
46. Ibid.
47. Ibid.
48. Quoted in Manchester, *American Caesar,* p. 76.

CHAPTER 4

49. Quoted in Manchester, *American Caesar,* p. 79.
50. Ibid.
51. Ibid.
52. MacArthur, *Reminiscenses,* p. 46.
53. Quoted in Blair, *MacArthur,* p. 18.
54. Ibid.
55. MacArthur, *Reminiscenses,* pp. 55–56.
56. Quoted in Blair, *MacArthur,* p. 18.
57. Quoted in MacArthur, *Reminiscenses,* p. 56.
58. Quoted in Manchester, *American Caesar,* p. 97.
59. Ibid.
60. Ibid.
61. MacArthur, *Reminiscenses,* p. 59.
62. Ibid., p. 67.
63. Ibid., p. 71.
64. Quoted in Blair, *MacArthur,* p. 21.

CHAPTER 5

65. Quoted in Perret, *Old Soldiers Never Die,* p. 114.
66. Ibid.
67. Quoted in Blair, *MacArthur,* p. 23.
68. Quoted in Manchester, *American Caesar,* p. 129.
69. MacArthur, *Reminiscenses,* p. 84.
70. Quoted in Manchester, *American Caesar,* p. 132.
71. Quoted in Blair, *MacArthur,* p. 25.
72. Ibid.
73. MacArthur, *Reminiscenses,* pp. 85–86.
74. Ibid., p. 87.
75. Quoted in Manchester, *American Caesar,* p. 141.
76. Ibid.
77. Quoted in Blair, *MacArthur,* p. 28.
78. MacArthur, *Reminiscenses,* p. 95.
79. Quoted in Manchester, *American Caesar,* p. 160.
80. MacArthur, *Reminiscenses,* p. 103.
81. Quoted in Blair, *MacArthur,* p. 37.
82. Quoted in Manchester, *American Caesar,* p. 164.
83. Quoted in Blair, *MacArthur,* p. 38.

CHAPTER 6

84. MacArthur, *Reminiscenses,* p. 106.
85. Ibid., p. 107.
86. Quoted in Blair, *MacArthur,* p. 43.

87. Quoted in MacArthur, *Reminiscenses,* p. 109.
88. Quoted in Manchester, *American Caesar,* p. 200.
89. Ibid.
90. Ibid.
91. MacArthur, *Reminiscenses,* p. 117.
92. Warren J. Clear, "The Gallant Defense of the Philippines," in Reader's Digest Association, *Reader's Digest Illustrated Story of World War II.* Pleasantville, NY: Reader's Digest Association, 1978, p. 152.
93. Quoted in Manchester, *American Caesar,* p. 215.
94. Ibid., p. 217.
95. Quoted in David G. Chandler, Colin McIntyre, and Michael C. Tagg, *Chronicles of World War II.* Godalming, UK: Bramley Books, 1997, p. 127.
96. Quoted in Manchester, *American Caesar,* p. 276.
97. Ibid., p. 275.
98. Ibid., p. 276.
99. Quoted in Blair, *MacArthur,* p. 81.

CHAPTER 7
100. Quoted in Costello, *The Pacific War 1941–1945,* pp. 225–26.
101. Quoted in Perret, *Old Soldiers Never Die,* p. 285.
102. Ibid., pp. 285–86.
103. Quoted in Costello, *The Pacific War 1941–1945,* p. 318.
104. MacArthur, *Reminiscenses,* p. 152.
105. Quoted in Thomas E. Griffith Jr., *MacArthur's Airman: General George C. Kenney and the War in the Southwest Pacific.* Lawrence, KS: University Press of Kansas, 1998, pp. 111–12.
106. MacArthur, *Reminiscenses,* p. 180.
107. Ibid.
108. Quoted in Ibid.
109. Ibid., p. 181.
110. Quoted in Perret, *Old Soldiers Never Die,* p. 386.
111. MacArthur, *Reminiscenses,* p. 185.
112. Quoted in Costello, *The Pacific War 1941–1945,* pp. 473–74.
113. Ibid., p. 474.
114. Quoted in Perret, *Old Soldiers Never Die,* p. 422.
115. Ibid., pp. 422-23.
116. Ibid., p. 423.
117. Ibid.
118. Ibid.

CHAPTER 8
119. Quoted in Blair, *MacArthur,* p. 227.
120. MacArthur, *Reminiscenses,* p. 271.
121. Quoted in Blair, *MacArthur,* p. 230.
122. Ibid., p. 231.
123. Quoted in Manchester, *American Caesar,* p. 448.
124. Quoted in Costello, *The Pacific War 1941–1945,* p. 601.
125. MacArthur, *Reminiscenses,* pp. 280–81.
126. Ibid., p. 282.
127. Ibid., pp. 282–83.
128. Quoted in Perret, *Old Soldiers Never Die,* p. 485.
129. Quoted in Manchester, *American Caesar,* p. 491.
130. Quoted in Blair, *MacArthur,* p. 249.
131. Ibid., p. 252.
132. Ibid., p. 253.
133. Ibid.
134. Quoted in John Bartlett, *Familiar Quotations: A collection of passages, phrases, and proverbs traced to their sources in ancient and modern literature.* 16th ed. Edited by Justin Kaplan. Boston: Little, Brown, 1992, p. 591.
135. Quoted in Blair, *MacArthur,* p. 255.

CHAPTER 9
136. MacArthur, *Reminiscenses,* p. 327.
137. Ibid.
138. Quoted in Bevin Alexander, *Korea: The First War We Lost.* New York: Hippocrene Books, 1986, p. 33.
139. Quoted in Robert J. Dvorchak and the Writers and Photographers of the Associated Press, *Battle for Korea: The Associated Press History of the Korean Conflict.* Conshohocken, PA: Combined Books, 1993, p. 14.
140. Quoted in MacArthur, *Reminiscenses,* p. 338.
141. Ibid., pp. 327–28.
142. Quoted in Dvorchak, et al., *Battle for Korea,* pp. 53-54.
143. MacArthur, *Reminiscenses,* p. 356.
144. Quoted in Alexander, *Korea,* p. 236.
145. Ibid., p. 237.
146. Ibid., p. 243.
147. Quoted in Harry G. Summers Jr., *Korean War Almanac.* New York: Facts on File, 1990, p. 298.
148. Quoted in Stanley Weintraub, *MacArthur's War: Korea and the Undoing of an American Hero.* New York: The Free Press, 2000, p. 312.
149. Ibid.
150. Quoted in Robert Leckie, *Conflict: The History of the Korean War.* New York: Da Capo Press, 1996, p. 268.
151. Ibid., p. 269.
152. Ibid.
153. Ibid., p. 270.
154. Quoted in Blair, *MacArthur,* p. 318.
155. Ibid., p. 319.

AFTERWORD
156. MacArthur, *Reminiscenses,* p. 400.
157. Ibid., p. 405.
158. Ibid., p. 426.

Alexander, Bevin. *How Great Generals Win*. New York: W. W. Norton, 2002.

———. *Korea: The First War We Lost*. New York: Hippocrene Books, 1986.

Ambrose, Stephen E., and C. L. Sulzberger. *American Heritage New History of World War II*. New York: Viking, 1997.

Bartlett, John. *Familiar Quotations: A collection of passages, phrases, and proverbs traced to their sources in ancient and modern literature*. 16th ed. Edited by Justin Kaplan. Boston: Little, Brown, 1992.

Bix, Herbert P. *Hirohito and the Making of Modern Japan*. New York: HarperCollins Publishers, 2000.

Blair, Clay Jr. *MacArthur*. Garden City, NY: Doubleday, 1977.

Caidan, Martin. *The Ragged, Rugged Warriors*. New York: Ballantine Books, 1972.

Chandler, David G., Colin McIntyre, and Michael C. Tagg. *Chronicles of World War II*. Godalming, UK: Bramley Books, 1997.

Coffman, Edward M. *The War to End All Wars*. The American Military Experience in World War I. Lexington, KY: University Press of Kentucky, 1998.

Connaughton, Richard. *MacArthur and Defeat in the Philippines*. Woodstock, NY: The Overlook Press, 2001.

Costello, John. *The Pacific War 1941–1945*. New York: Quill, 1982.

Dear, C. B., and M. R. D. Foot, eds. *The Oxford Companion to World War II*. New York: Oxford University Press, 1995.

Dupuy, R. Ernest, and Trevor N. Dupuy. *The Encyclopedia of Military History: From 3500 B.C. to the Present*. Rev. ed. Harper & Row, Publishers, 1986.

Dupuy, Trevor N., Curt Johnson, and David L. Bongard. *The Harper Encyclopedia of Military Biography*. New York: HarperCollins, 1992.

Dvorchak, Robert J., and the Writers and Photographers of the Associated Press. *Battle for Korea: The Associated Press History of the Korean Conflict*. Conshohocken, PA: Combined Books, 1993.

Editors of Time-Life Books. *WW II: Time-Life History of the Second World War*. New York: Barnes & Noble, 1995.

Eggenberger, David. *An Encyclopedia of Battles: Accounts of over 1,560 Battles from 1479 B.C. to the Present*. New York: Dover Publications, 1985.

Eisenhower, John S. D., with Joanne T. Eisenhower. *Yanks: The Epic Story of the American Army in World War I*. New York: Free Press, 2001.

Fehrenbach, T. R. *This Kind of War: The Classic Korean War History*. Washington, DC: Brassey's, 1994.

Flanagan, E. M. Jr. *Corregidor: The Rock Force Assault, 1945*. Novato, CA: Presidio Press, 1997.

Griffith, Thomas E. Jr. *MacArthur's Airman: General George C. Kenney and the War in the Southwest Pacific*. Lawrence, KS: University Press of Kansas, 1998.

Hallas, James H. *Doughboy War: The American Expeditionary Force in World War I*. Boulder, CO: Lynne Rienner Publishers, 2000.

Leckie, Robert. *Conflict: The History of the Korean War*. New York: Da Capo Press, 1996.

———. *The Wars of America. Vol. 2: From 1900 to 1992*. New York: HarperCollins, 1992.

MacArthur, Douglas. *Reminiscenses: General of the Army Douglas MacArthur*. Annapolis, MD: Naval Institute Press, 2001.

Manchester, William. *American Caesar: Douglas MacArthur 1880–1964*. Boston: Little, Brown, 1978.

McClain, James L. *Japan: A Modern History*. New York: W. W. Norton, 2002.

Milner, Samuel. *Victory in Papua: United States Army in World War II: The War in the Pacific*. Harrisburg, PA: National Historical Society, 1993.

Morison, Samuel Eliot. *Leyte: June 1944–January 1945*. Vol. 12. History of United States Naval Operations in World War II. Edison, NJ: Castle Books, 2001.

———. *The Liberation of the Philippines: Luzon, Mindanao, the Visayas: 1944–1945*. Vol. 13. History of United States Naval Operations in World War II. Edison, NJ: Castle Books, 2001.

Morton, Louis. *The Fall of the Philippines*. United States Army in World War II: The War in the Pacific. Minnetonka, MN: National Historical Society, 1995.

Nalty, Bernard C., ed. *War in the Pacific: Pearl Harbor to Tokyo Bay*. London: Salamander Books, 1999.

Perret, Geoffrey. *Old Soldiers Never Die: The Life of Douglas MacArthur*. Holbrook, MA: Adams Media, 1996.

Polmar, Norman, and Thomas B. Allen. *World War II: The Encyclopedia of the War Years 1941–1945*. New York: Random House, 1996.

Reader's Digest Association. *Reader's Digest Illustrated Story of World War II*. Pleasantville, NY: Reader's Digest Association, 1978.

Rice, Earle, Jr. *Strategic Battles in the Pacific*. San Diego, CA: Lucent Books, 2000.

Spector, Ronald H. *Eagle against the Sun: The American War with Japan*. New York: The Free Press, 1985.

Summers, Harry G., Jr. *Korean War Almanac*. New York: Facts on File, 1990.

Toland, John. *In Mortal Combat: Korea, 1950–1953*. New York: William Morrow, 1991.

———. *No Man's Land: 1918, The Last Year of the Great War*. New York: Ballantine Books, 1980.

———. *The Rising Sun: The Decline and Fall of the Japanese Empire 1936–1945*. 2 vols. New York: Random House, 1970.

———. *But Not in Shame: The Six Months after Pearl Harbor*. New York: Signet Books, 1962.

Weintraub, Stanley. *MacArthur's War: Korea and the Undoing of an American Hero*. New York: The Free Press, 2000.

Beasley, W. G. *The Japanese Experience: A Short History of Japan*. Berkeley, CA: University of California Press, 1999.

Bergamini, David. *Japan's Imperial Conspiracy*. New York: Pocket Books, 1972.

Bergerud, Eric. *Fire in the Sky: The Air War in the South Pacific*. Boulder, CO: Westview Press, 2000.

———. *Touched with Fire: The Land War in the South Pacific*. New York: Viking, 1996.

Blair, Clay. *The Forgotten War: America in Korea 1950–1953*. New York: Times Books, 1987.

Boyne, Walter J. *Clash of Wings: Air Power in World War II*. New York: Simon & Schuster, 1994.

Cowdrey, Albert E. *Fighting for Life: American Military Medicine in World War II*. New York: The Free Press, 1994.

Craig, William. *The Fall of Japan*. New York: Galahad Books, 1997.

Cutler, Thomas J. *The Battle of Leyte Gulf 23–26 October 1944*. New York: Harper-Collins, 1994.

Davis, Paul K., *100 Decisive Battles: From Ancient Times to the Present*. New York: Oxford University Press, 1999.

Dower, John W. *Embracing Defeat: Japan in the Wake of World War II*. New York: W. W. Norton, 1999.

Edgerton, Robert B. *Warriors of the Rising Sun: A History of the Japanese Military*. New York: W. W. Norton, 1997.

Edwards, Bernard. *Salvo! Classic Naval Gun Actions*. London: Arms and Armour, 1995.

Ferguson, Ted. *Desperate Siege: The Battle of Hong Kong*. New York: Doubleday, 1980.

Flower, Desmond, and James Reeves, eds. *The War, 1939–1945: A Documentary History*. New York: Da Capo Press, 1997.

Frank, Richard B. *Downfall: The End of the Imperial Japanese Empire*. New York: Random House, 1999.

Gibney, Frank. *The Pacific Century: America and Asia in a Changing World*. New York: Charles Scribner's Sons, 1992.

Gilbert, Martin. *The Second World War: A Complete History*. New York: Holt, 1989.

Goulden, Joseph C. *Korea: The Untold Story of the War*. New York: Times Books, 1982.

Jablonski, Edward. *Airwar*. Vol. II. Garden City, NY: Doubleday, 1971.

Jansen, Marius B. *The Making of Modern Japan*. Cambridge, MA: The Belknap Press of Harvard University Press, 2000.

LaFeber, Walter. *The Clash: A History of U.S.–Japan Relations*. New York: W.W. Norton, 1997.

Lamont-Brown, Raymond. *Kamikaze: Japan's Suicide Samurai*. London: Arms & Armour Press, 1997.

Lewis, Jon E., ed. *The Mammoth Book of Eye-Witness History*. New York: Carroll & Graf Publishers, 1998.

———. *The Mammoth Book of Battles*. New York: Carroll & Graf Publishers, 1995.

Library of America, The. *Reporting World War II, Part One: American Journalism 1938–1944*. New York: Library Classics of the United States, 1995.

———. *Reporting World War II, Part Two: American Journalism 1944–1946*. New York: Library Classics of the United States, 1995.

Miller, Nathan. *War at Sea: A Naval History of World War II*. New York: Scribner, 1995.

———. *The Naval Air War 1939–1945*. Annapolis, MD: Naval Institute Press, 1991.

Moskin, J. Robert. *The U.S. Marine Corps Story*. 3rd rev. ed. Boston: Little, Brown, 1992.

Prange, Gordon W., with Donald M. Goldstein and Katherine V. Dillon. *Miracle at Midway*. New York: Penguin Books, 1982.

———. *At Dawn We Slept: The Untold Story of Pearl Harbor*. New York: McGraw-Hill, 1981.

Reynolds, Clark G., and the Editors of Time-Life Books. *The Carrier War*. Alexandria, VA: Time-Life Books, 1984.

Sides, Hampton. *Ghost Soldiers: The Forgotten Epic Story of World War II's Most Dramatic Mission*. New York: Doubleday, 2001.

Smith, Patrick. *Japan: A Reinterpretation*. New York: Pantheon Books, 1997.

Wheeler, Richard. *A Special Valor: The U.S. Marines and the Pacific War*. New York: Harper & Row, 1983.

EARLE RICE JR. is a former senior design engineer and technical writer in the aerospace industry. After serving nine years with the U.S. Marine Corps, he attended San Jose City College and Foothill College on the San Francisco Peninsula. He has devoted full time to his writing since 1993 and has written more than forty books for young adults. Earle is a member of the Society of Children's Book Writers and Illustrators; the League of World War I Aviation Historians and its U.K.–based sister organization, Cross & Cockade International, the United States Naval Institute, and the Air Force Association.

CASPAR W. WEINBERGER was the fifteenth secretary of defense, serving under President Ronald Reagan from 1981 to 1987. Born in California in 1917, he fought in the Pacific during World War II then went on to pursue a law career. He became an active member of the California Republican Party and was named the party's chairman in 1962. Over the next decade, Weinberger held several federal government offices, including chairman of the Federal Trade Commission and secretary of health, education, and welfare. Ronald Reagan appointed him to be secretary of defense in 1981.

During his years at the Pentagon, Weinberger worked to protect the United States against the Soviet Union, which many people at the time perceived as the greatest threat to America. He became one of the most respected secretaries of defense in history and served longer than any previous secretary except for Robert McNamara (who served 1961–1968). Today, Weinberger is chairman of the influential *Forbes* magazine.